Rome for Food Lovers

PETER LOEWE

Hardie Grant

TRAVEL

CONTENTS

LEGEND

- **O** Opening hours
- **A** Address
- **T** Telephone
- **W** Website
- **E** Email
- ***i*** Information

The height of happiness: a yellow
Rome-registered Fiat 500

INTRODUCTION

ROME – *PASTA NON BASTA!*

"You're writing a restaurant guide? Why? Everything is on the internet these days!"

My friend smiled at me, slightly mocking and triumphant.

If writing this book has taught me anything, though, it's how big the need is for authentic guide books where the authors have actually been to, and eaten at, all the places reviewed. Today anyone can be a food critic and share their experiences and ratings online. Some of these reviews can certainly be very professional.

While writing this book, I clearly saw how certain restaurants that in my opinion are consistently some of the best were left out or given unreasonably bad reviews. The economic interests at play in a city like Rome, with millions of visitors each year, are enormous. Not everyone in the industry is serious or loyal to their colleagues. Not everyone follows the philosophy that a publican once shared with me: "A serious pub has no rivals, only colleagues".

In this guide, I haven't given any ratings for the places I have reviewed; I haven't included any places that, for various reasons, haven't been good; and many restaurants that could have been included in this book haven't been, due to lack of space and time. The only conscious choice I made was to not include any places that have been awarded a star by the *Michelin Red Guide*. Those with Michelin stars are already easy to find because they're in all the guides, but importantly, these elegant dining experiences are often indistinguishable – no matter how well you eat when you go to these restaurants, you could have the same experience whether you're eating in New York, Stockholm, Paris, London or Berlin.

But a Roman trattoria exists only in Rome!

You may notice that many of the eateries in this book are a good distance from the city center. I have consciously sought out the best culinary experiences in Rome's outskirts, because today many of the best, and above all most authentic, eateries lie outside the city center. Roman culinary traditions and family recipes are better preserved here than in the center where too many places have adapted opening times, food and prices to suit the city's large stream of visitors.

Certain places are marked with a lion; these are places that offer something that goes beyond just fantastic food and makes for an unmissable experience: staff, decor, tradition or a unique history that feels truly alive.

I am faithful to my favorite haunts, so the chances that we'll run into each other at one of the trattorias in this book are fairly good.

Peter Loewe

IT STARTED WITH WINE

In Rome the white wine flows, light and dangerously easily. At a simple neighborhood pub you can still order *un quartino* (a small quarter-liter carafe) for 3–4 euro. Or go for a half or *un litro*. Sneaky, because it's often inferior wine that wasn't bottled.

In ancient times the wine was dragged into town on carts. At the city port San Giovanni, sales were swift. The wine came in earthenware amphorae, which were unloaded in Rome, adjacent to the river. So many amphorae were unloaded here that over the centuries a whole mountain of discarded pottery quickly formed. Of course, other things like olive oil and grain also contributed to the mountain of piled-up *testae* (shards) until it finally reached a height of 115 feet (35 meters). Today this pottery mountain has given its name to this part of town, Testaccio.

Today Rome's wine comes from the villages south of the city, Castelli Romani (the Roman castles), like Frascati, Marino, Albano and Velletri. White wine made from Malvasia grapes dominates.

Rome's restaurant tradition began with wine; it was all about small places (**Cantina Cantarini** from 1903 is the best preserved example, p. 19). At lunchtime workers would come to these places that Romans called "a hole in the wall". Here they were served chilled wine and, if they were lucky, there was also fresh bread, but people often brought their own lunches. Some workers came with no food at all, and so the wine places began to throw together a pasta, the simplest imaginable, like *ajo, ojo e peperoncino* – pasta tossed with oil, garlic and a bit of chili pepper.

A few of these places still remain. They are called *cantina* (wine cellar) or *osteria* (referring to the host, *oste*). A version with "h" occurs also, but a *hosteria* can also be an upscale guesthouse. A *bottiglieria* takes its name directly from the bottle, while a *fiaschetteria* refers to the famous

Chi mangia pane campa, chi beve vino non muore.

Those who eat bread live, those who drink wine never die.
Italian proverb

Possibly Rome's creamiest *carbonara* at Hostaria Romana Boccaccio (p. 72)

fiber-wrapped bottle *il fiasco* – a Tuscan tradition from the 1300s; it's associated with Chianti, but was in style earlier in the capital as well.

Rome's restaurant boom occurred at the end of the '50s. Economic stability had slowly been re-established after the difficult war years. In the beginning of the '60s, the city was invaded by workers from southern Italy. Rome's administration, authorities and government ministries, and a construction boom drew people to the city. Among them were many men, who had never cooked before, who left their wives and children at home with hopes of earning more money to support them.

An eatery opened in nearly every central quarter then, and in many popular areas there were several. In these years, the small family restaurants were all in the city center. These are known as *la trattoria* – a Roman institution that should be World Heritage listed because it's quickly disappearing. Places where regular customers could dine on credit, as Ettore Scola so lovingly depicts in his bittersweet film *We All Loved Each Other So Much*.

In the wine district around Frascati the wine bars were called *frasca* and they had a bough outside to identify them. The host provided the wine and the guests brought their own food. It's been ten years since the last proper *frasca* closed, when Armandone died. Armandone would open his *frasca* at the end of the year when his wine was ready to drink. Late in the summer, when the wine was gone, he closed. He served only wine he made himself. This tradition is now lost and the places that today call themselves *frasca* are ordinary tourist restaurants.

As late as the '60s it was still normal for Romans to go to an *osteria* and bring food with them from home. Especially in the working quarter Testaccio, once dominated by Mussolini and fascism's *case popolari* (public housing), going down to the corner pub with your own food was a common practice. Better than sitting home alone with a plate of *bucatini all'amatriciana* – at the *osteria* it was warm and there were friends and musicians who passed by and sang for a plate of pasta.

This tradition died out as the world became more commercialized. During the '70s, with the city shuddering from the activities of the terrorist organization the Red Brigades, and also a rise in kidnappings, street crime and fascism, it wasn't particularly nice to go out in the evening – it was safer to eat at home.

IN A ROMAN BELLY

A proper Roman eats most things. Offal in general is a specialty. A whole lamb's head that's split down the middle and roasted in the oven with potatoes and rosemary is considered a treat for many Romans. Another is deep-fried lamb brains with artichokes or *coratella* (a mix of lamb lung and spleen).

In Rome there was a big celebration when veal intestines became legal again. *Pajata*, the superb Roman dish that's cooked in a rich tomato sauce and served with ribbed macaroni, has a creamy flavor from the milk that's left over inside the calf's intestines and which curdles during the cooking. It's about as far as the Roman kitchen is prepared to stretch, when it comes to using milk and cream in cooking.

Intestines were banned when mad cow disease broke out in the '80s. It was probably some food authority in the government who thought the dish was so distasteful and therefore took the opportunity to ban all sales. It was

Rigatoni con pajata (pasta with veal innards)

misguided, because the regulation applied to animals older than 18 months and not suckling calves, from which *pajata* is made.

Another popular dish, *coda alla vaccinara* (oxtail), isn't really offal. The dish requires 4–5 hours slow cooking so the meat falls easily off the bone. It is cooked in tomato sauce with lots of celery and a touch of grated dark chocolate. *Schienali* (grilled spinal cord) with melted butter and sage is also a delicious and ancient dish.

In Rome you're never quite sure what you're eating. The most remarkable ingredients are covered in tomato sauce and grated cheese, or finely sliced into a cold salad. *Nervetti*, a cold or lukewarm salad of cartilage, is eaten throughout Italy. It's proof of their ingenuity in cooking, and the belief that absolutely every part of an animal should be used.

Other gastronomic specialties are tongue, sweetbreads, calf-foot and *trippa* (tripe). Tripe should ideally look a little yellow or slightly gray; if it's a pretty white

it has been bleached before cooking. And there's *le palle* (testicles), which on menus has the dangerously indecipherable name *granelli* (grain).

The risk of being served bull testicles isn't too high, though. People in Rome say it's a dish that only butchers' children eat. But at **Betto e Mary** (p. 18) the dish is almost always on the menu. My friend ordered it once – thinly cut, breaded and fried meat slices which looked like miniature Wiener schnitzel, so soft and tender that it melted in the mouth without any obvious flavor. Everyone at the table wanted to taste it too, without knowing what it was. When my friend finally revealed the secret ingredient, everyone was shocked.

Offal is most popular in Testaccio which, until 1975, had Rome's biggest slaughterhouse. The tradition of eating offal, though, is centuries old. In earlier times the nobility and high-ranking members of the Catholic Church (the pope and the many cardinals) took the best cuts of meat. The people had whatever was left over. So rose the concept of *il quinto quarto* (the fifth quarter) – something that doesn't exist in mathematics. These are cuts with special flavor or lots of bone and little meat that Roman housewives transformed into major gastronomic delights.

Rome's other food tradition comes from the city's Jewish quarter. Here deep-fried dishes are common, and the showpiece is the Jewish artichoke – a very tricky dish. Artichokes are best at the beginning of spring when they aren't too big. They must be rinsed properly and the largest leaves taken off. The difficulty lies in timing the frying perfectly so that the bottom of the artichoke becomes soft in the oil, while the leaves should become crispy like chips, without getting burned. It's a dish that must be timed down to the second. Of course Romans deep-fry all kinds of vegetables – yellow zucchini blossoms are delicious filled with mozzarella and anchovies, dipped in batter and fried.

FINDING YOUR WAY IN THE CITY

Rome is big. In area it's about ten times larger than Paris! The distance from north to south is 30 miles (50 kilometers). Up until 1993 the municipality was even larger, but then Fiumicino, which lies next to the Tyrrhenian Sea, became its own municipality. The city's large airport, Leonardo da Vinci, is also in another municipality.

Pecorino Romano from Antica Caciara in Trastevere (p. 164)

To explain which area or quarter an eatery lies in isn't easy. The city famously has seven hills, which historically were major geographic markers. There are no restaurants around the two historic hills Capitoline and Palatine, but there are restaurants on the hills Esquiline near Roma Termini, and Viminal, today synonymous with the ministry of the interior in the same way that the hill Quirinal is linked to the presidential palace. The green hills Aventine and Caelian lie adjacent to the Colosseum. The hills aren't particularly useful when you're trying to find the location of a certain pub or bistro, except for Esquiline, where there are masses of restaurants.

Another issue is that Romans don't understand borders. Rome has around 22 quarters, called *rioni*. One quarter is giant, the others teeny-tiny. In the book's geographic descriptions I name the quarters, like Trastevere, Testaccio, Monti, Prati, Borgo (adjacent to the Vatican) and sometimes Campo Marzio (the marching field where the military exercises were held in antiquity). But very few Romans know where the other quarters start and end – like Colonna, Ponte, Parione, Regola, Sant'Eustachio, Pigna, Campitelli, Sant'Angelo, Ripa, Ludovisi, Sallustiano, Castro Pretorio, San Saba and Trevi – though it is actually easy to find out. The quarters are numbered, so get a full numbered list of the 22 quarters. On the white street signs which are placed on corner buildings, under the street's name there's a letter R followed by a Roman numeral; this numeral lets you know which quarter you're in. The areas that came after *rioni* are quite neatly called *quartieri* (neighborhoods). Most Romans know these more common neighborhood names.

In this book, I've opted to be practical. "Center" refers to the city's historic center, the heart of city. On the other side of the Tiber River, I use neighborhood names like Trastevere, Borgo and Prati. When I go into the outskirts of the city, I often refer to the road names: Tiburtina, Tuscolana, Prenestina, Casilina and more. And so you don't get completely lost, I've also included descriptions of how to get to each of the eateries.

IV TAXIS AND BUSES

It is still quite cheap to take a taxi in Rome, which is good to know if you'll be going to authentic eateries outside the city center. There are several taxi companies: Cooperativa 3570 is the biggest, phone: 06 3570 (the area code always needs to be included); or Samarcanda, phone: 06 5551 or 06 6645. You can also ask the restaurant to help you order a taxi.

There's a set fare for a taxi to and from both airports in Rome: 48 euro to Fiumicino and 30 euro to Ciampino. The price covers up to four people and includes baggage. Drivers also can't add an extra late-night or Sunday fee. At Fiumicino the drivers follow the set prices, but at Ciampino it can be difficult to get a taxi if you point out that the price is 30 euro.

Trains to and from the airport are cheaper. Express trains to Roma Termini cost 14 euro and take 30 minutes. Local trains to Roma Termini cost 8 euro and stop at other stations such as Trastevere, Ostiense and Tiburtina. At the last two you can transfer to the metro. Note that the last train from Fiumicino to Roma Termini leaves as early as 11.23pm.

The cheapest way to get to Roma Termini is to take a bus for 4–5 euro. There are night buses, but they don't run often (www.cotralspa.it). At night, taxis are your best bet!

From Ciampino there's no direct train service, but buses go to Roma Termini and cost 4–5 euro. You can also take a city bus to Anangina and then take the metro – it's the fastest way to get into town if you land in the morning or early afternoon, when trains into the city can take a long time. Bus 720 is new and connects Ciampino with metro B (the blue line) – the station Laurentina goes to Roma Termini; this trip in or out to Ciampino costs 1.50 euro and takes about an hour.

Asking your hotel to book a taxi is generally more expensive. They often use the private service, NCC (car with chauffeur), and the porter takes a fee. It's possible to pre-book a taxi to Roma Termini and then to the airport. All taxis in Rome are white and are available if the sign is lit. It's fine to hail a taxi on the street, however, never accept any taxi offer when the taxi queue is long. These are illegal black cabs and can be both expensive and dangerous.

ATAC is the company that runs Rome's metro and buses. For a capital city, Rome's public transportation is poorly developed. Bus tickets cost 1.50 euro and are good for 100 minutes but only for one trip on the metro. There are also day tickets for 7 euro, three-day tickets for 18 euro and week-long passes for 24 euro. Bus services start at 5.30am and the last bus leaves the terminal at midnight. The metro's last trip is at 11.30pm, but it's extended to 1.30am on Fridays and Saturdays.

A tavola non s'invecchia

At the table, no one grows old

RBS 6 NAZIONI 2008
STADIO FLAMINIO · ROMA

BIRRA
PERONI

PERONI
La Birra Ufficiale della
Nazionale Italiana di Rugby

JOHN
HANCOCK

PUNTABOUT

CHE LA FORZA SIA CON NOI.

The finishing touch on a spaghetti *cacio e pepe* is made directly in a hollowed-out pecorino romano cheese by Ilaria Di Pietro at Trattoria da Danilo (p. 43)

TRATTORIAS

What distinguishes a trattoria from a restaurant? There's not an obvious answer. The word's origins are unclear. There may be a link to the French word *traiteur*, but the word doesn't really directly translate. A proper trattoria exists only in Italy, and no other city has as many as Rome. A trattoria is a typical little neighborhood bistro, nearly always family-owned, with daily specials. The cook devotedly takes care of his regular customers and already knows beforehand what they will order and how they like their dishes cooked. Trattorias are the social hub of any authentic neighborhood, where people meet and chat, or drop in to say hi and knock back an espresso at the counter. Or, after they put away the groceries at home, they slouch in, exhausted, and beg to take home a couple of servings of chicken and some broccolini fried in garlic and chili. This is the kind of place where it really pays to be a regular!

It's no exaggeration to say that trattorias are endangered. Many places have started to remake themselves; traditional paper table coverings and harsh fluorescent lights are becoming increasingly rare. Admittedly it is nice to eat in a more pleasant atmosphere, but in conjunction with renovations, the prices go up, while the menus tend to shrink. Authentic neighborhood trattorias with fair prices are unfortunately becoming all too rare.

When I came to Rome it was still normal for the owners of a trattoria to offer guests a *digestivo*, usually a bitter amaro meant to promote digestion. This started because the restaurateur would have a guilty conscience after having served so much food, because a trattoria doesn't know what *nouvelle-cuisine* portions are. It often happened that, after dinner at my neighborhood pub along Appia Nuova, you'd get four bottles full of vodka, grappa, amaro and *limoncello* (lemon liqueur). My Swedish friends sat and gaped when I explained that this was free. And the waiter was in no hurry to take the bottles away from the table. This tradition today is wholly gone, since the alcohol tax has gone up even in Italy. But a glass of amaro might still be offered after your *cena* (dinner).

Italy remains a measurement-free land when it comes to alcohol and drinks. If I'm in Stockholm and order a Campari soda and get the standard question, "How many centiliters should it be?" I would be completely stumped and have to change my order to a glass of wine.

Today not all trattorias are simple and cheap. Some are more upscale but continue to call themselves "trattoria"; Trattoria Monti (p. 45) is a shining example.

ANTICA ROMA

If a *camion* (truck) manages to get up a small road it would be a victory for the driver. In Italian, large portions of food are called *da camionista* – if you eat everything, it's a victory for your digestive system. Antica Roma is a glutton's paradise, but even so it wouldn't be worth writing about if the food wasn't also really good.

I like to come here on a hot summer evening. On the hill Monteverde you're 650 feet (200 meters) higher up, and the air feels cooler. All the pasta dishes are good – the best is probably *spaghetti allo scoglio* with tomatoes, mussels, clams and shrimp. Even the meat dishes are excellent, like *saltimbocca alla Romana* (veal with prosciutto and sage) or deep-fried lamb cutlets served with deep-fried artichokes. I don't recommend pizza here though.

In summer the outdoor seating is open, and the place can be packed both inside and out, so you might wait a long time for a table. My advice is to book a table when the place opens at 7.30pm.

Take bus 75 from Roma Termini or from the bus stop Morosini (Trastevere) toward Poerio to the bus stop Barrili. Note that it takes 30 minutes from Roma Termini, but only 11 from Trastevere. Return buses go from the adjacent Via Poerio.

- Ⓞ *Open evenings only, every day except Wednesday*
- Ⓐ *Via Alberto Mario 17A–B; Monteverde Vecchio*
- Ⓣ *+39 06 581 6809 or +39 34 772 11171*

BETTO E MARY

This faintly anarchistic joint has a cult following, not least because multiple journalists from the TV company RAI have made it their regular haunt. Signs on the walls with statements like "Neckties absolutely forbidden" and "Here we serve only mad cows" set the tone. This is the workers' neighborhood Mandrione.

In summer it's best to eat outside, though the decor mostly resembles a garden shed with old tools. Here you can indulge in offal of all kinds. There's a tasting plate for those who want to try the full range: intestines, lungs, liver and tripe. It's helpful to know that *granelli* are testicles. But don't worry – they don't come to the table unless you order them specifically. There are also classier meat cuts grilled over an open flame. Pork and sausages don't cross the threshold, but horse meat does.

The narrow-gauge train from Via Giolotti takes you out to Via Casilina and to many of the book's most iconic eateries

The place has looked the same in the decades since Benedetto and Maria opened it. Today it's their son Tommy Spoletini who sits down at the table and goes through the menu with his hoarse voice in a Roman dialect. The house's *tonnarelli* (egg pasta) with *animelle* (sweetbreads) and artichokes is an excellent start. An authentic eatery, with few foreign visitors and plenty of red wine flowing.

Take the narrow-gauge train from Roma Termini along the far end of Via Giovanni Giolitti; get off at the bus stop Filarete.

O *Open every day except Sunday*
A *Via dei Savorgnan 99; Mandrione – along Via Casilina*
T *+39 06 647 71096*

 CANTINA CANTARINI
Photographs on the walls show how this little place looked in the early 1900s. Not much has changed in 100 years. The paper table coverings are still here, as well as wooden chairs and harsh overhead lighting. Still, the comfort level is high. That is mainly due to the staff. Nello Pieretti – a waiter here for over half a century – believes that "the waiter's profession is the finest there is, because you have so many friends from all corners of the world who often come back". Trust Nello when he asks: *Faccio io?* That means he will serve you a selection of the day's starters. Many of them he made himself, while Luigi Brunori cooks the main courses in the tiny kitchen.

Go here particularly when they serve fish – their best dish. From an Italian herring tray and marinated little fish to *nero di seppie* (coal-black cuttlefish spaghetti), or a sauté of different kinds of mussels. Their *fritto misto* (mixed-fry platter) is a classic. The humble setting belies the fact that there are often ultra fresh oysters, large shrimp and even lobster to enjoy. The dishes are priceless in their simplicity and unparalleled in all of Rome. Fish is served Thursday evening, and for lunch and dinner on Friday and Saturday. At other times only meat dishes are available. All the dishes reflect the family's roots in the Marche region of Italy.

O *Open every day except Sunday*
A *Piazza Sallustio 12; Ludovisi-Via Veneto – near Via XX Settembre*
T *+39 06 485 528 or +39 06 474 3341*
W *www.ristorantecantinacantarini.it*

Oven-baked fish with crispy potato
skins at Dal Ragioniere (p. 21)

Fritto misto at Cantina
Cantarini (p. 19)

DAL CAVALIERE GINO

On a small street with minimal signage just behind the parliament building is this little pearl. The wall murals are terrible 1970s kitsch, but you get used to them. Rome works that way; family traditions are preserved on the walls. Today it's Gino's children who run the place: Carla and Fabrizio. The dishes remain unchanged. *Tonnarelli alla Ciociara* is a square, flat spaghetti noodle with mushrooms, smoked pork and peas. The waitstaff here still grate fresh pecorino or parmesan cheese on to your pasta until you're satisfied – a nice gesture that has almost wholly vanished from Italy's restaurant world.

The *i secondi* (main course), is the best, especially the oxtails or beef roulade. Both are cooked slowly in a thick tomato sauce. They go well with perfectly roasted potatoes or *puntarelle* (salad greens) with oil, garlic and anchovies. Rabbit cooked in wine or braised beef with tomatoes and onion *alla picchiapò* are other unusual dishes to try. Don't leave without peeking into the kitchen. In the midst of the gratins and casseroles is a splendid ancient granite column that is attributed to the famous Baroque architect Gian Lorenzo Bernini – Gino's kitchen, several hundred years ago, must have been part of a large inner

courtyard that disappeared during the remodeling of this old building.

 Open every day except Sunday; no credit cards accepted

Ⓐ *Vicolo Rosini 4; Center*

Ⓣ *+39 06 687 3434*

___

DAL RAGIONIERE

This restaurant is a reliable gem for those who want to eat good fish and seafood pasta. The founder Leonardo Anzuini has left, but the style and genuine commitment to quality food remains. Today it's Leonardo's son Ercole – owner of Rome's most stylish mustache – who runs the kitchen, while Leonardo's daughter Daniela serves. Start with a sauté of Rome's best and largest mussels or have the house-special fish *zupetta* (soup) with mussels, shrimp, fresh

AREA CODE 06

Note! When you are in Rome you don't have to dial the country code +39. All landline numbers however must begin with the area code 06, or else the number won't work. (This doesn't apply to cellphone numbers.)

baby tomatoes and toasted bread. Nearly all the pasta dishes are perfect, like the *bavette alla pescatora* (shellfish pasta), or clams with truffles. But even the *carbonara* rises well above the average Roman level.

Fish like *spigola* (sea bass) or *orata* (often sold as sea bream) are baked and served in a very refined style: when the fish is cooked through, all the bones are taken out; the fish, which has kept its form, is then covered with a thin layer of potatoes that are perfectly crispy; a dish worth waiting for. In terms of the food in general, you get good value for money here. The house's bottled wine from Zagarolo outside of Rome isn't something you'll remember for the rest of your life, but it's inexpensive and pleasant enough. If you're after a better wine, there are only a few bottles to choose from.

Take bus 105 from Roma Termini to the bus stop Tor Pignatara.

O *Open every day except Sunday and Monday*
A *Via Gerardo Mercatore 7; Marranella – near Via Casilina*
T *+39 06 243 03599*

DA CESARE AL CASALETTO

This is a restaurant for the summer months. The charm of the place is that you can settle in on the large veranda that is covered with grapevines. The decor is not especially picturesque. There's an air of the early '60s around the place: Marmite floors with chipped limestone and metal chairs to sit on – pretty comfortable! The food is simple and very well prepared. Little croquettes of eggplant, crispy on the outside, tender inside, with an aftertaste of mint and drenched in one of the city's heartiest tomato sauces, are a good start. As are fried zucchini flowers with anchovies. Classic pasta dishes,

Ercole Anzuini

say with mussels and grated pecorino, bear witness to the kitchen's Neapolitan inspiration. You choose which sort of pasta you'd like with the various toppings on order. The pizza is zingy and perfect. The baker overturns all theories that you must have a wood-fired oven to make good pizza.

The new managers, who took over in the past few years, understand the value in both keeping the showpiece dishes and introducing something new – like fried gnocchi served with cheese and black pepper. The place is open year-round, but indoors is the modern Cesare which isn't quite as appealing. Although it's far from the center, it's easy to get here with tram 8 from Piazza Venezia to the end-station Casaletto. The place is across the street. Definitely worth making the journey.

O *Open every day except Wednesday*
A *Via del Casaletto 45; Monteverde Nuovo*
T *+39 06 536 015*
W *www.trattoriadacesare.it*

DA ENZO AL 29

When it comes to the interior, nothing here has changed. The walls are still a light sulfur-yellow, tubes of fluorescent lights still hang from the ceiling and the paper table coverings are still in place – although they're now checked. But food-wise, a lot has happened in a few years. I like the creamy, lightly salty shredded burrata called *stracciatella* with fresh sweet tomatoes as a starter. The fried zucchini blossoms are light and have, of course, not been frozen, and the mozzarella filling is soft and appealingly stringy; but above all, the flowers are salty from the sardines that these days are often missing from this

dish – they are an expensive ingredient. In the middle of autumn I order fettuccine with asparagus – delicious and fresh despite being out of season. I've also tried *le polpette di coda*, fried meatballs made from oxtail and cooked in tomato sauce; the meatballs sit like gems on top of the dark tomato sauce and parmesan, and a sprinkling of cocoa on the rim of the plate is reminiscent of the tradition of having chocolate in the sauce when you cook oxtail. A perfect and sinfully good dish that I'd never eaten before!

Since my first visit Enzo has rightly become a cult-favorite. And foreigners have caught on. Book well ahead because the place is tiny. Also, because of its size, Enzo doesn't take bookings of more than six people. There are no bookings at lunch, and only one booking for 7.30pm, when you have to arrive on the dot to get your

Filleted and marinated *alici* at Dal Ragioniere (p. 21)

table. And the whole group has to be there! Those who arrive after 10pm can just slip in – if there's anything left to eat!

O *Open every day except Sunday*
A *Via dei Vascellari 29; Trastevere*
T *+39 06 581 2260*
W *www.trattoriadacesare.it*

DA NERONE

There are places with an appeal that goes far beyond the food; they represent something unique and irreplaceable. So it is with this trattoria which for more than 50 years has been run by Eugenio de Santis. His sister Adele runs the kitchen. To see how the head waiter, Theo, carries out one table after another onto the sidewalk on a warm summer evening as regular guests arrive is a rare and wonderful sight.

At Nerone not much has changed since the 1930s. The food is simple. Start with their enormous buffet of small appetizers. But note that it doesn't work like a smorgasbord; you can help yourself to an ample serving, but only once! After

that, I recommend a pasta. Nerone has Rome's best *spaghetti alle vongole* (clams), cooked perfectly al dente, with the freshest clams and mussels that taste of the sea – just right – with garlic, parsley and a hint of chili. Adele knows very well that this dish should never have a sea of oil in the bottom of the plate, which happens at all too many places. Their egg pasta *da Nerone* with ham, salami, mushrooms and peas is a good option too. The *carbonara*, though, isn't quite creamy enough. The house wine holds up.

You can happily sit for a long time on the sidewalk of this quiet street on the hill Colle Oppio just above the Colosseum. Very few cars pass by and no street musicians wander past. This is truly an authentic hidden corner in the Eternal City.

O *Open every day except Sunday*
A *Via delle Terme di Tito 96; Colle Oppio*
T *+39 06 481 7952*

DAR FILETTARO A SANTA BARBARA

An institution, with a slightly threadbare and kitschy decor; even calling this place a trattoria would once have been a serious exaggeration. Previously, the restaurant served only fried fish fillets as *baccalà* (salted cod) and, at most, fresh broadbeans when they were in season. These days there's even pecorino cheese and the classic curly salad sprouts, *puntarelle*, with anchovies. The real revolution is that there's now bottled wine and even dessert. But the dry cakes, like *ciambelle* (biscotti) and *tozzetti* (nut biscuits), to dip in the house malvasia wine, are of course still here.

Romans love this disorderly little place, where the TV comes on the moment any

Eugenio de Santis at Da Nerone

Dar Filettaro is located in a small square near Campo dei Fiori (p. 24)

soccer match starts. Many come in just to buy a takeaway fish fillet. In summer the place spreads out into the car-free square along Via dei Giubbonari. One of the few authentic places that remain around Campo dei Fiori.

O *Open every day except Sunday, 5.30–11pm*
A *Largo dei Librai 88; Center*
T *+39 06 686 4018*

DA SETTIMIO

Thanks to a good friend, a few years ago I met one of Rome's major restaurant personalities: Signora Carla Cremonese; to all customers she's just Carla. All year she dresses in black pants with a low-cut top, like a teenage girl

⌄ **At Dar Filettaro they serve, among other things, fried *baccalà* (salted cod) (p. 24)**

even though it's been a good while since she passed 60. For a long time she's run Da Settimio, and says emphatically, "I cook my grandmother's food". Same recipes, same care. The menu is posted outside, but it doesn't come to the table. Instead Carla sits down with the customer at the table and carefully goes through the entire menu in a Roman dialect – fast-paced English is also available.

Start with her *tavolozza* plate with cold cuts from Umbria: perfectly soft salami and lightly peppery air-dried ham. The kitchen is small and everyone at the table must agree on one shared pasta. It may be rigatoni in tomato sauce cooked with the house oxtail – a distinctly meaty flavor, well balanced with celery, fills the palate. As a regular customer I have always enjoyed Carla's simple main dishes: lamb stew *alla cacciatore*; her butterfly-light

^ **Signora Carla Cremonese, one of Rome's major restaurant personalities**

fried *polpette* (meatballs), which are really more like tiny hamburger patties; and her outstanding *spezzatino* (stew) made with pork and green peas. And it all happens in a tiny space that's always packed full.

It's absolutely necessary to book a table, especially in the evenings around 8pm. It's located to the side of the Portuense quarter. Take bus 44 from Via del Teatro di Marcello, adjacent to Piazza Venezia. But with Carla's low prices you can afford a taxi.

O *Open every day except Monday*
A *Via di Val Tellina 81; Portuense – near Piazza Scotti*
T *+39 06 582 30701*

FIASCHETTERIA BELTRAMME

Since it opened in 1886 a whole world has passed through this little place near the Spanish Steps. First and foremost were the artists, who ate on credit and paid with a painting – the place has been protected as a historical building since 1980, so the art cannot be moved. Directors like Fellini and Pasolini have discussed scripts and films while eating here. And I myself have sat at the same table as the actor Vittorio

Gassman – because the tables are for four people, you often end up sharing.

The restaurant has had a new manager for the past couple of years. Tradition is preserved, but these days the kitchen is better than it's been for many decades. That's true of the classic spaghetti dishes like *carbonara*, but also creative dishes like mushroom ravioli in a walnut sauce.

The daily special is nearly always best, and as rule there's always a fish dish. The dessert we tried – cheesecake with blackberries and strawberry coulis – was relatively large. But it was so good that we deeply regretted the decision to share one portion between us. Points off for the house red wine, though. The straw-wrapped vessels that gave this place its name now stand museum-like on shelves. Ask for bottled wine instead.

The place has Tuscan roots and was started by Beltramme Moscardini. It got its nickname in the early 1900s, when the culture was dominated by the idea of futurism. The owner was large and, legend has it, not exactly beautiful. The nicest thing you could say about him was that he was *bello come un tram* (as pretty as a tram). And thus he became Beltramme.

For a long time this was a Swedish hangout. Look for the drawing of a group of naked ladies walking – *Swedes in Rome* is the title. How exactly it got its name is impossible to find out. Maybe it happened when Anita Ekberg took the Roman nightlife by storm? To my knowledge she hasn't been here, but Madonna has, to eat pasta, when her film *Evita* premiered in Rome. Researchers from the Swedish Institute have eaten here for decades, as did the Swedish king Gustaf VI Adolf. At that time, regulars had their own linen napkins that were kept in a cupboard with

their own napkin rings. Thus a foreign ambassador might have his linen napkin while his guest, a king, made do with a paper napkin.

These days everybody gets a proper napkin. Beltramme remains a place where good food and unique restaurant history meet. Most of the guests are Italian, which says everything about the place's standing in this quarter. It is, however, more expensive than an ordinary trattoria.

 *Open every day for lunch and dinner*
Via della Croce 39; Center
+39 06 697 97200

FRANCESCO ER LAZIALE
There aren't too many trattorias in Rome like this one. And to find them these days, you have to go deep into the city's outskirts. The Angelini family's simple, precise cuisine is worth the trip, by bus or by the old narrow-gauge train that ends at Roma Termini station along Via Giovanni Giolitti – the stop is *stazione* Laziali.

Here the whole family cheers on the Lazio football team, but it isn't really a sports bar. You immediately meet the friendly, flirtatious Antonella who serves and makes the desserts. Mamma Antonietta runs the kitchen with her son Marco. Nothing has changed since father, Francesco, left the scene in 2007. All the traditional pasta dishes are here. Try Antonietta's *trofie* (macaroni from Liguria) with pancetta and zucchini, which even includes the yellow flowers. It tastes homemade and rich, without being drenched in oil or covered in butter. Antonietta's chicken *alla cacciatore* is a showpiece. The high quality meat is purchased from a local butcher in the Centocelle neighborhood.

The place wins praise also for its *i contorni* (vegetable sides). There's always broccoli rabe, cauliflower, grilled peeled peppers and *saltato* (bitter chickory salad) with oil, garlic and chili. And considering that it's a simple trattoria with wood paneling, kitschy art and Padre Pio on the walls, the fine gray linens and starched napkins on the table are surprising. The house wine does just fine.

🅞 *Open every day except Wednesday all day and Sunday evening*
🅐 *Via Casilina 493; off Via Tor Pignattara*
🅣 *+39 06 241 3229*

———

HOSTARIA FARNESE

For years I walked past this small place with its anonymous entrance. "It couldn't actually be anything good, here in the midst of Rome's absolute worst tourist traps", I thought – Hostaria Farnese is located precisely between the once very picturesque square Campo dei Fiori and Piazza Farnese. I wish I had known better! Behind this anonymous entrance hides some of the city's best food. I've enjoyed perfect artichokes *alla Romana* and, after that, a large piece of juicy lamb, warm and crispy fresh out of the oven. Unfortunately in Roman restaurants, lamb is often made in advance and can be a little sad and dry when served quickly warmed up. That's not how it is here.

Other dishes the place is known for are egg-pasta fettuccine with artichoke, and spaghetti with mussels and small tomatoes. The pastas come with plenty of grated pecorino according to Neapolitan tradition, which freely blends fish and cheese. It works well in these dishes.

We said "No" to a dessert that was the most egg-yolky tiramisu I have ever seen in my life. How it tastes, you'll have to find out for yourself.

The place is, of course, family-owned. Since 1964 Francesco and Maddalena Contini have run it. Today it's their eminent, smiling son Luca who manages the business. It's a wonder that the place has remained unchanged. Dear readers, the place is a treasured secret, so don't spread it around.

🅞 *Open every day except Thursday*
🅐 *Via dei Baullari 109; Center*
🅣 *+39 06 688 01595*

———

LA CAMPANA

On the marching field where, in antiquity, Rome's soldiers held their military exercises lies the city's oldest restaurant. La Campana (the church bell) is noted in a *taxae viarum* (tax record) from the year 1518. It said that a certain Pietro della Campana that year had paid six scudi in tax for his *osteria*, which at that time in addition to serving food also functioned as a postal station with rooms for travelers and a place to refresh your horses.

For more than 100 years the Trancassini family has run the place. Historic restaurants can make visitors uncertain about authenticity, but here you can relax. This is a classic little old-fashioned place with good traditional food.

One or two dishes stand out, like the *broccoli e arzilla* (pasta soup) with a noticeable fish flavor from rockfish cut into small pieces. The *melanzane alla Parmigiana* (eggplant gratin) which is cooked in the oven with tomato, mozzarella and parmesan, is also quite good. Their showpiece is *la vignarola*. This is a soup made with the first spring vegetables from the garden plot – in olden times it was the first vegetables that matured in the farmer's *la vigna* (wine field), because at that time people grew other crops between the rows of wine grapes, hence the dish's name. *Vignarola* is made with artichoke, broadbeans, fresh peas, spring onions and flavorful meat. The dish seems to be at La Campana year-round, but of course with frozen ingredients. You should eat this in spring (April or May) and then you'll understand how La Campana has managed to survive for 500 years.

- **O** *Open every day except Monday*
- **A** *Vicolo della Campana 18; Center – Campo Marzio*
- **T** +39 06 687 5273
- **W** *www.ristorantelacampana.com*

LA SAGRA DEL VINO
In one corner of the heavily trafficked Via Medaglie d'Oro lies La Sagra del Vino. The name can be translated as "wine party". The place still has the original tiles, now covered in countless stickers.

At least on paper, these days it's son Valentino Rovazzani who's in charge. But happily his father, Candido, is still serving and taking care of the regulars. In the kitchen is Candido's wife, Marcella, called Lella by everyone. This guarantees that the simple Roman dishes, like *pasta e fagioli* (pasta with beans), are made with enormous care. The same is true of the main dishes, like *trippa*, meatballs, oxtail and the house lamb.

There's no written menu. Candido tells you what's available and suggests what you should eat. The house wine is always good. Meals conclude with *ciambelle* (biscotti) that you dip into the house wine. It's worth seeking this place out because it's one of the city's most authentic kitchens, serving true Roman flavors. There are outdoor tables in summer. The place is 10 minutes from the metro stop Cipro.

- **O** *Open every day except Saturday and Sunday*
- **A** *Via Marziale 5; Balduina*
- **T** +39 06 397 37015

LA TAVERNACCIA DA BRUNO
This historic trattoria has been refurbished with modern, bright furnishings, but had the sense to keep its menu the same. You should begin with their charcuterie served with perfect freshly baked focaccia. Follow with one of their pasta dishes or soups. We were blessed with the egg pasta with wild boar and even happier with the suckling pig with crispy rind, cooked in a wood-fired oven, as is their lamb. The wine list is long and good, but the house red and white wine are also available – something that is increasingly rare at newly-opened restaurants. Finish with the homemade chocolate cake or mousse. Or try the famous *tartufo* ice-cream from Pizzo Calabro in Calabria – it's industrially produced, but very good. Choose from dark chocolate, pistachio or licorice – a Calabrian specialty.

Here you quickly and happily become a regular, not least because of the care and personal service that characterizes the Persiani family, who have run the place for decades.

It's in Trastevere, but far from the quaint tourist zone. Here you're in the area that's known for the big market Porta

Portese which runs on Sundays. Bus 170 or tram 8 will get you close.

(O) *Open every day except Wednesday*
(A) *Via Giovanni da Castel Bolognese 63;
Trastevere – near the train station*
(T) *+39 06 581 2792*
(W) *www.latavernaccia.com*

LO SGOBBONE

Orderly and authentic, this neighborhood restaurant upholds tradition and quality. The day's dishes are written up on a blackboard. We ate a perfect soup with brown beans and pasta, then the house egg-pasta pappardelle with mushrooms. As a main dish we chose *spezzatino di vitello* (veal stew) that melted in the mouth. The homemade *visciole* (pie of ricotta and amarelle) was an excellent finish. Fish dishes are few and served only on Fridays. In autumn, I especially recommend the pasta *al tartufo* – thin egg pasta comes generously covered in thin slices of black truffle. It's one of the simplest and most delicious dishes you can get in Rome.

Sgobbone can perhaps be translated as "worker ant", here personified by the owner Filippo di Placidi, who everyone knows as Pippo. Pippo has owned the place for more than 30 years. This little neighborhood bistro is tucked away in the neighborhood Flaminio, just over a mile (2 kilometers) from Piazza del Popolo. Take tram 2 from metro stop Flaminio to the end station Mancini.

(O) *Open every day except Sunday*
(A) *Via dei Podesti 10; Flaminio*
(T) *+39 06 323 2994*

LO SPUNTINO

It looks like a faded cafeteria, a *tavola calda* as they're called in Italy. Few would be inclined to stop in, and I must admit that I would sometimes go to the little Thai place across the street without even noticing Lo Sputino. But my friend Maria Valeria recommended it to me, and guaranteed that it would be a culinary delight. So I stepped into this simple little place and sat at a table.

Luigi Mancosu cooks food from his home of Sardinia. There are many Sardinian restaurants in Rome, but few that I return to time and again. Here, there's no menu. The friendly Luigi tells you what's available, and you don't have to think about the prices. We tried his unique gnocchi with clams and *bottarga*; unique in that it is three-colored – the colors of the Italian flag. Each gnocco has one bit of plain, uncolored dough, one bit that's green with parsley and one bit that's red from carrots. It not only looks great, but also tastes great. A typical Sardinian specialty is the small grain *fregola* that swells when cooked. They're eaten with clams, which the Sardinians call *arselle*. It can be like a soup, but here it's nearly like loose couscous made of pasta grains cooked al dente. Thinly sliced tomatoes and saffron complete the dish.

You can also get the day's fresh fish here, but following a recommendation, I ate the grilled, thinly sliced octopus that's been finished in a pan with artichokes.

Eat a couple of dishes and, if you complement them with wine (there's no set etiquette here), the bill will come to around 50 euro for two. That's hard to beat in Rome when you eat seafood! If you're lucky, the owner offers his homemade myrtle liqueur or *amaro Luigia*, which he also makes himself from a secret recipe. Signor Luigi is often the only waiter and has a cook in the kitchen.

I recommend that you go here Tuesday, Wednesday, Thursday or Sunday evenings. Avoid Friday and Saturday, when it can be busy and the kitchen sometimes has trouble making the dishes perfectly. The place also serves pizza, but that's not the right choice here. In the summer, there are a few tables outside to enjoy your meal.

Take bus 44 from Marcellus Theater, adjacent to Piazza Venezia, to bus stop Bottazzi right by the restaurant. In the evenings tram 8 runs frequently; get off at Piazza San Giovanni di Dio. You'll arrive at Lo Sputino after about five minutes' walk down Via Ozanam.

O *Open every day except Monday*

A *Via Federico Ozanam 109;*
Monteverde Nuovo

T *+39 06 535 501*

L'OSTERIA DI BIRRA DEL BORGO

This small brewery, founded by the beer enthusiast Leonardo di Vincenzo, has been much buzzed about. Even more so after it was recently bought by the world's largest brewing company, the Brazilian-Belgian Anheuser-Busch InBev. In a strong economy, Birra del Borgo opened this elegant beer hall–restaurant in the Prati neighborhood. Of course, here the wine is overshadowed by the beer.

Above the chrome counter are an amazing 24 glimmering beer taps; half of which are the brewery's own beers. For thirsty beer lovers, coming here on a warm summer day is akin to going to the brewery world's Sistine Chapel. The extremely enthusiastic and knowledgeable staff let you taste-test the various beers if you aren't sure what to choose. The menu is fairly beer-oriented, where the pizza portions are tailor-made by pizza guru Gabriele Bonci (p. 109). Here he revives Rome's classic pizza crust that's cut in half

Regulars can have their name on a table at
Osteria dell'Angelo (p. 35)

and stuffed with delicious fillings such as artichoke and prosciutto or creamy *burrata* and is served in pairs with spicy salami. Even classic, relatively fancy pizza comes in slices. Groups can order a large sampler plate to share, with five different sorts of pizza for around 25 euro. Of course there's also bruschetta, cheeses, cold cuts, pasta and the day's special, like oven-baked chicken in stew. All of it in a fun, modern, specially designed space.

Ⓞ *Open every day 12pm–2am*
Ⓐ *Via Silla 26; Prati*
Ⓣ *+39 06 837 62316*
Ⓦ *osteria.birradelborgo.it*

OSTERIA BONELLI

This is a relatively new family eatery along Via Casilina, the ancient road that today is home to many of Rome's most authentic restaurants. Osteria Bonelli is always packed, even though the place is big. A board with the day's many dishes is brought to your table. There is usually antipasti to begin with, like fried salted cod or radicchio gratin from Treviso with grated grana (a parmesan-like cheese that's made in a considerably shorter time). We led with a perfect charcuterie plate, even as we cast longing glances at the fried artichokes that were being served at the neighboring table. Continue with the fish soup with broccoli, cheese and sprinkled black pepper – an old Roman dish. I've never eaten a better one than here. Calf liver from a *vitella* (heifer), melted in my mouth, while my friends enjoyed the house pomodoro-drenched meatballs served with fresh stuffed zucchini. We couldn't manage a dessert, but the restaurant offered us an *amaro*.

The street outside is a huge square full of parked cars, even in summer, unfortunately. This now slightly obscure suburban neighborhood is anything but new; the restaurant is named after an ancient aqueduct, Acqua Alexandrina, built in the year 226 AD.

You must book several days in advance to get a table, especially on Friday and Saturday. It's best to book for early afternoon or for 7pm, before the place is invaded by loyal regulars. It's good value.

Take the local train to Roma Termini on Via Giovanni Giolitti to Centocelle. Get off at Berardi station and then it's a five minute walk.

Ⓞ *Open every day except Sunday*
Ⓐ *Viale dell'Acquedotto Alessandrino 168–180; Alessandrino – along Via Casilina*
Ⓣ *+39 32 986 33077*

OSTERIA DELL'ANGELO

For lunch you can order what you'd like à la carte. But in the evenings a set menu is served for 25 euro. Some simple and delicious starters arrive, and you choose what you want for the rest of the meal: classic Roman pasta dishes like a perfect *carbonara* or an unusual ribbon-spaghetti with tomato sauce and anchovy fillets. The main dishes are the best: the house meatballs, oxtail rolls or rabbit in white wine with herbs. You may also choose the house vegetables, like spinach, artichoke or broccolini, to accompany your main.

The dishes vary from day to day. All are extremely fresh and well made. There is no tourist menu; this is where the Prati neighborhood's regulars eat. For more than 30 years the place has been run by former rugby player Angelo Croce. The walls are full of countless sports photos and trophies. Next door is the well-known Teatro dell'Angelo, a performing arts theatre that is also named after the restaurant's owner. The restaurant is large and it's relatively easy to book a table.

- ⓞ *Open every day except Saturday lunch and Sunday*
- Ⓐ *Via Giovanni Bettolo 24; Prati*
- Ⓣ *+39 06 372 9470*

OSTERIA DELLA SUBURRA

Suburra was not exactly a nice neighborhood in Rome's early days – it was home to dodgy wine bars and numerous brothels. This was the underworld, below the hills Quirinal and Viminal, hence the name "suburbs". Today the area is called Monti and has been my home neighborhood for more than 20 years. It's now become quite trendy. Many new places have opened, but sadly I've been pretty disappointed by the quality.

This *osteria* is the safest bet if you want to go to a simple, straightforward restaurant. The menu is enormous. The house antipasti is good, especially the veggie version, *ortaggi nostri*. Homemade wide pappardelle with ragu of wild boar appears on the winter menu, as well as a version with broccoli, pork and pecorino. The *cinghiale alla bracconiera* (wild boar stew) is also very good. *Coratella* is the city's classic offal stew of lamb liver and lung cooked in white wine – a delicious dish that has become all too rare.

This is also one of few city restaurants that always offers *lumache* (snails) – something Romans traditionally eat only around midsummer. The snails are smaller than French ones, but much better, in thick tomato sauce with mint and chili. It's an effort to eat them with a toothpick. This is

not a seafood restaurant, but the *spaghetti al nero di seppie* (black squid pasta) is a safe choice. Inside, the decor is spartan and not particularly warm and welcoming, so the outdoor tables fill up first and they, unfortunately, cannot be booked.

- ⓞ *Open every day except Monday*
- Ⓐ *Via Urbana 67; Center – Monti*
- Ⓣ *+39 06 486 531*

QUI SE MAGNA

At the end of the long Via del Pignetto lies this authentic little eatery, where the name in Roman slang translates best to "There's grub here". In the early days, the name signaled that this was a place where you could also eat – this simple suburban neighborhood is dominated by bars and humble wine huts that didn't typically serve food. Qui Se Magna was run for decades by the charismatic Valeria Pallagrosi who was always in the kitchen. These days her children Paolo and Pina have taken over.

All of the classic Roman dishes remain, for the most part, but the menu has been refreshed. Some of the new dishes include a satisfying potato souffle with chickpeas and a hint of ginger, and the very good *polpettone* (meat stew) in red wine sauce. Those who are seriously hungry should try the house gnocchi with meat ragu or *in bianco*, as it's called in Italian when the dish doesn't include tomatoes. At this restaurant they also serve gnocchi with cheese and walnuts.

The house white and red wines from Marino are very simple and inexpensive. Try a quarter liter and then inevitably you'll end up ordering a bottled wine, with the average price around 14 euro.

Taking Metro C to the station Malatesta is the easiest way to get here.

O *Open every evening except Sunday and Monday, lunch only on Sunday*
A *Via del Pignetto 307A; Pigneto*
T *+39 06 274 803*

_____

RISTORANTE S. ANNA

This restaurant, located in a small alley, looks a bit sleepy and drab at the outset – it has wood paneling on the walls and the standard checked tablecloths. But this eatery is an absolute find, in terms of the quality of the meat and fish, the superb customer service, and the inexpensive prices. A sauté of clams and *cozze* (mussels) arrives as a huge mountain, ultra fresh and with exactly the right amount of oil, chili and garlic. The portion size kept me busy for 20 minutes and cost 9 euro. In any other neighborhood, a dish like this would probably cost at least twice as much and be half the size. My *rombo* (plaice), oven-baked with thinly sliced potatoes, was also enormous. The waiter came and showed off how much I'd finished before he cleared my plate.

This eatery also has some adventurous pasta dishes, risotto and various starters, including a rich cheese plate. There's pizza made by a professional baker – which proves that the dough is so infinitely much more important than whether the pizza is baked in a wood-fired oven or, as here, an electric oven.

There are restaurants that have low meal prices but then make up for it with higher drinks prices. Here, wines by the glass go for 4 euro: three red wine options and three white wine options. Mineral water costs 1.50 euro for a half-liter and 2 euro for a whole liter – evidence of this restaurant's overall integrity.

O *Open every day except Sunday*
A *Via di Sant'Anna 8–9; Center – near Largo di Torre Argentina*
T *+39 06 683 07190 or +39 06 689 6485*
W *www.ristorantesantanna.it*

_____

SORA LUCIA

This little trattoria has grown since it opened in this new location in 2018. But in all the imporant ways, it remains the same. In the past, fish dishes dominated the menu almost completely. Today a series of classic meat dishes like oxtail in a perfect tomato sauce have also appeared, along with *polpette* (meatballs). The best choice is the daily special, listed on the blackboard. I often choose my favorite pasta, *linguine al principe* – "the prince's" thin ribbon spaghetti that consists of fresh small tomatoes served with shrimp, squid and mussels. Those who are regulars will recognize some changes. In 2018 the charismatic mamma Signora Liliana who cooked here for decades passed away. But her son Simone Nardocci maintains the place's traditions.

Notice the bullet holes that remain along the street's facades. Via Rasella was the site of an attack by the Italian resistance against an occupying German battalion on 23 March 1944. Thirty-three Germans died. In retaliation, the following day the Germans rounded up and shot 335 Romans who had no connection with the attack.

O *Open every day*
A *Via Rasella 138; Center – near Via del Tritone*
T *+39 06 679 4078*

_____

Amatriciana, the famous pasta dish from north Lazio

WHY AREN'T ITALIANS FATTER?

I remember how I spent one of my first evenings living in Rome. It was the middle of the 1980s; I was in the outdoor seating area at a well-known restaurant located just a stone's throw from the Piazza Navona. At the next table over was a young Italian couple clearly in love; the young man had obviously invited his girlfriend out for a feast. Maybe he was rationing his pennies, and that's why he didn't eat much himself, but the wafer-thin Italian girl's eating habits impressed me. First, she devoured sliced ham with melon, then a large mountain of pasta and then an enormous piece of meat with specially ordered vegetables. She didn't even skip dessert, though now I forget what it was.

This raised an interesting question for me: how is it that Italians aren't fatter?

Italians do exactly the opposite of what all the nutritionists advise: they start the day with a cup of black espresso and, at most, a *cornetto* (croissant). Adults generally don't eat a midday meal; although lunch is more common now that the practice of midday siesta has vanished. Lunch (if it's eaten) is then followed by a hearty dinner feast each night; often three courses. In short: after this meal you're still full when you wake up in the morning.

However, working in their favour, Italians have moderate alcohol consumption. And dessert isn't big in Rome and may be replaced with ice-cream; but often you're so stuffed when you've finished eating that you skip dessert altogether.

HOW MUCH SHOULD YOU ORDER?

At the time that I was studying Italian in Rome, I got a furious look from a waiter when I asked for the *il conto* (check) after having ordered only one dish. These days no one expects you to eat three dishes. Or really to eat much more than antipasti, *primo e secondo*, *contorni* as a side, and then fruit, cheese and *dolce*.

Ok, now I'm exaggerating; that's more like a wedding in Sicily.

But it's still regarded as rather uncouth to order only a pasta, especially at dinner. A solitary main course is always ok, but the Italian kitchen beckons you to eat more. Combine your pasta with a small starter, or a vegetable afterward, or a dessert, and you will have behaved absolutely correctly by Italian standards.

VII HOW TO AVOID TOURIST TRAPS

Eateries that are purely tourist traps are on the increase, especially in the city center, but they're easy to recognize. Restaurants with a person outside shouting to beckon you in should be avoided. These types of places are usually found around the Pantheon, Piazza Navona and the Vatican.

Look at the menu posted outside. Do they have typical Roman dishes or other regional dishes? Or do they offer only cold cuts, cheese, salad and hamburgers? In that case, they may not even have a chef or a proper kitchen, just pre-cooked pasta dishes warmed in a microwave by a waiter.

If the place has a special tourist menu for 15 euro with two dishes and a dessert, you should be suspicious. Generally, the risk of disappointment is high. The same is true if an eatery seems unrealistically cheap. If you can get a dish for 5–6 euro at a restaurant (there are such places in Trastevere) you should ask yourself where the ingredients come from and what the working conditions are like in the kitchen.

Opening times are also a clear indicator. A restaurant that is open the whole afternoon is probably geared to tourists – the food can still be good, of course; but it isn't a place for Romans, who are discerning and know how things should taste. Romans eat lunch between 1 and 3pm and dinner from 8pm but in summer they don't turn up before 9pm at the earliest. A restaurant that is packed at 6pm makes me hesitate; and if a place is totally quiet at 9pm, that's also a sign something is wrong.

The hardest places to judge are ordinary restaurants that don't have the menu outside, and which might even have white curtains in the window so you can't look in. For many people, if they can't see menu prices, they think it will be an expensive, upscale restaurant. But that might not be the case. Be brave, step inside and see what it looks like first. Ask for a menu: *Posso vedere il menu?* Anonymous entrances can disguise some really great eateries with amazing food. These are the types of places that already have a steady stream of contented regulars. **Perilli** in Testaccio (p. 86) is an excellent example.

VIII TIPPING

Romans are economical with tips. Some restaurants still add an extra *coperto* (cover charge) to the bill, even though this has been abolished. Therefore you may pay for your bread basket instead. A very proper restaurant will ask these days if customers would like bread – although honestly this doesn't happen often. If a *servizio* (service charge) is added, you usually don't leave a tip, nor if it's a classic family bistro.

In other cases, though, such as at a trattoria, it's customary to round up the bill with 1–2 euro per person. If you don't, it signifies that you were unhappy with the meal. Just remember, you can't leave a tip when you pay with a credit card in Italy.

SORA MARGHERITA

From the outside, this place resembles a broom closet. There's no sign, but a large collection of people hovering on the street outside, waiting for a table, lets you know that you're in the right place. Sora Margherita has been here since the 1920s. Back then, it was a wine bar with a daily pasta on offer. In the '60s it expanded; the adjacent church Santa Maria del Piantos' sacristy was absorbed by the restaurant and became a dining room – a very Roman solution! Thanks to Lucia Ziroli the place has continued to thrive, continuing the work of the legendary Margherita Tomassini who revived the eatery after 40 years of neglect.

Time seems to have stood still here. Each morning Lucia makes her own pasta. All the tables in the dining room are covered with large balls of egg-yolk dough.

By lunchtime they have been transformed into the day's tortelloni or fettuccine. Here they adhere strictly to tradition: on Fridays they serve *baccalà* (dried cod in tomato sauce) and on Saturdays *trippa* (tripe) with tomato sauce sprinkled with mint and grated sheep's cheese.

The place is in the middle of the Jewish quarter. This means no pork in the meat sauce and no ham in Lucia's roulade, which instead is filled with chopped egg. Book ahead, but don't come too late!

Ⓞ *Open for lunch every day, except Sunday in summer; for dinner every day except Tuesday and Sunday (only Sunday in summer) – two evening bookings, 8–9.30pm and 9.30–11.30pm*

Ⓐ *Piazza delle Cinque Scole 30; Center*

Ⓣ *+39 06 687 4216*

_____

TRATTORIA DA DANILO

You really don't want to arrive here too late. Those who arrive first get the best tables, as long as you've booked ahead. Otherwise, you have little chance of being lucky enough to eat at this little restaurant, unless you want to eat in the cellar which isn't quite as cozy.

Danilo Valente runs this place – one of the city's best neighborhood bistros – and mamma Pina is in charge of the kitchen. The decor is simple, with wood veneer and a lot of photographs of famous customers on the walls. The food is of a high quality and characterized by Roman culinary staples. The house *carbonara* alone, which you can also have with shaved black truffle (and also white truffle in autumn) makes it worth a weekly pilgrimage here. The other pasta dish, *cacio e pepe* (cheese and black pepper) is thrown together before the guest's eyes in a huge hollowed-out wheel of pecorino cheese. Even the raw beef is chopped and shaped in front of the guests. Danilo also serves a delicious lamb.

To start with, the house's fun charcuterie plate is a good choice. To finish, the dessert *gasperino* is something all dessert addicts should order. Similar to a trifle, the dessert comes in a large glass, and is filled with pastry and fresh ricotta mixed with chopped chocolate, chantilly cream (which in Italy is a mix of whipped cream and vanilla cream) and a few drops of the fancy dessert wine *passito* from the island Pantelleria. You are in paradise!

O *Open every day except Sunday all day and Monday lunch*
A *Esquiline – adjacent to Piazza Vittorio; Emanuele*
T *+39 06 772 00111*
W *www.trattoriadadanilo.com*

TRATTORIA DA LUIGI

In the city center, Da Luigi holds its own in this little square along Corso Vittorio Emanuele II, near Chiesa Nuova. The square has two restaurants, both with large outdoor seating areas. Da Luigi is clearly the best.

You shouldn't expect any creative, complicated dishes here, but everything is done with precision. Here they don't fry the golden zucchini blossoms filled with mozzarella, but rather grill them – a specialty *alla balestra*. My spaghetti *alle vongole* was delicious and the house *vitello tonnato* was perfect.

They still do the classic papal pasta dish *paglia e fieno alla papalina* here; it's a mix of gold and green egg pasta called straw and hay, served with peas, mushrooms and cream. This dish, still made in Trastevere, was eaten by cardinal Eugenio Pacelli who soon became Pope Pius XII in 1939.

Regulars often say the meat dishes are a stronger option than the fish. Beef *alla Fiorentina* proves this, as does the grilled veal cutlets or the fried cockerel, *galletto alla diavola*.

In summertime it's always packed, mostly with foreign visitors. At one of the tables I've seen Rome's 'King of the Paparazzi', photographer Rino Barillari. He nearly always eats alone. He comes here after finishing his work because the food is good, and because in his game, the really big celebrities that he wants to photograph don't go to Da Luigi.

- **O** *Open every day except Monday*
- **A** *Piazza Sforza Cesarini 23–24; Center – along Corso Vittorio Emanuele II*
- **T** *+39 06 686 5946*
- **W** *www.trattoriadaluigi.com*

TRATTORIA DER PALLARO

For many decades, in the square outside of this historic trattoria you would encounter Giovanni Fazi, who would shout at and pounce on potential customers. He would roar in Italian: "Do you know this place and know that you cannot choose anything?" If he got no answer he would shout, "*Se ne vada!*" (Away with you!) Many customers became confused enough they took his advice and left. Today the elderly Giovanni sits quietly outside and lets his wife, whom all know as Signora Paola, handle the business, which also includes the food in the kitchen.

The point of Giovanni's shouts was that here you never know what you're going to get. It is rather nice to be able to just sit yourself down and not have to make any choices or think about what you feel like eating. Normally they serve antipasti with ham, salami, mozzarella and little fried rice balls. Last time of I was there, I had divine lentils that reflected Paola's origins in north Lazio, where the lentils from Castelluccio, in the Apennine Mountains, are famous. Then followed a combo of two types of pasta: rigatoni *alla carbonara* and a choice of *amatriciana*, *gricia* or *cacio e pepe*.

Fish is extremely rare, even on Fridays. As a main dish, generally there's beefsteak or a meat stew of veal with vegetables. The meal finishes with a piece of cake and a little liqueur, provided you behaved appropriately, which is to say eaten up most of everything. If not, Paola can give guests very disapproving looks, and you might think she's serious, but her smile is never gone for very long!

Everything, even the wine, is included in the price, which varies between 25–30 euro. It can be less if, for example, you skipped the pasta. The many outdoor tables usually fill up first.

O *Open every day for lunch and dinner*

A *Largo del Pallaro 15; Center*

T *+39 06 688 01488 or +39 33 053 9657*

TRATTORIA LILLI

You could live in Rome for many years without ever passing by this trattoria on a hidden street in the city center. This well-respected eatery is favored by Romans, especially in winter.

The trattoria's namesake, Lilli Ceramicola, is 85 years old and retired. The trattoria is run by her children Patrizia, Dino and Silvio who preserve the memory of her husband Angelino's food.

It's all about simple dishes. Start with their antipasti with mozzarella and Parma ham. The *amatriciana* is excellent, as is the house ravioli filled with ricotta and spinach, served with sage and butter.

In winter there's *bollito* (boiled beef) with green sauce, which is also served in a tomato sauce of onion, garlic and herbs, *alla picchiapò*, as this ultra Roman dish is called. This dish was originally created as a way to serve leftovers.

The best dish is probably the chicken *alla cacciatore* (hunter style) in white wine with vinegar, rosemary and a few anchovies. Homemade desserts are also available. Trattoria Lilli is very good value for being in the city center.

O *Open every day except Sunday evening and Monday*

A *Via di Tor di Nona 23; Center – Campo di Marzio*

T *+39 06 686 1916*

W *www.trattorialilli.it*

TRATTORIA MONTI

A rustic little neighborhood bistro that soars high above all the other trattorias thanks to its impeccable service and friendly staff, plus the sophisticated dishes that, even on my first visit, stood out as culinary works of art. Begin with the *tortino* (oven-baked casserole) – it's like a delicious bed of of red onion and mild gorgonzola sauce. Continue with the house *tortello* made of fresh egg-pasta filled with ricotta and spinach. Inside, there's a runny egg yolk that seeps out when you put your fork into it. In autumn the dish is sprinkled with white truffle.

Other main dishes are roulade of swordfish, breaded lamb cutlets with fried zucchini or sliced warm carpaccio of duck breast with orange sauce.

Desserts are a must. The lightly frozen ice-creams with almond biscuits are served with chocolate sauce and are seriously addictive. Similarly the apple

Roulade of eggplant, ...

... *tortello* with spinach, ricotta and egg yolk

... poached *baccalà* with asparagus

... and pear tarte tatin at Trattoria Monti (p. 45)

cake is delcious, served with the creamiest *zabaione* (Italian custard dessert) I've ever eaten.

The place has been run by the same family from the Marche region for decades: mamma Franca Marziani holds court in the kitchen while sons Enrico and Daniele serve.

Bookings are recommended; regulars who haven't booked wait outside at 11pm in hopes of being let in. It can often be a long wait though, because you'd happily spend a long time sitting in this trattoria, enjoying a grappa after dinner.

O *Open every day except Sunday evening and Monday*
A *Via di San Vito 13A; Esquiline – between Santa Maria Maggiore and Piazza Vittorio Emanuele*
T *+39 06 446 6573*

TRATTORIA MORGANA

This little trattoria on a quiet central side street is one of the cutest things I've seen. The waiters carry out tables one after another and set them directly on the sidewalk – which actually is not allowed anymore. But very few cars pass by here, so at Morgana the tradition is still carried out for nearly half the year.

After repeated visits I noticed that Morgana had recently refreshed its menu with several new dishes. Try the cheerful *fusilli* (spiral macaroni) with clams, sardines and *cime di rape* (delicate green broccoli from Apulia). Here the classic bean soup *pasta e fagioli* gets a maritime revamp with the addition of mussels, clams and little octopuses. *Straccetti* is shredded steak flash-fried in a pan, served with pine nuts and currants. The house *baccalà* is made in the oven with tomatoes,

capers, black olives, onion and oregano. For those who want classic Roman dishes, there is *trippa* (tripe), wild boar, *lumache* (snails), oxtail and of course the housemade potato gnocchi with tomatoes and melted gorgonzola.

The wine list has changed and become national, with high-quality wines from all over Italy. But there's still the good house wine, sold by the carafe, whole, half or a quarter liter. You can also just order a single glass for 3 euro, and it is large.

O *Open every day except Wednesday*
A *Via Mecenate 19–21; Esquiline – along Via Merulana*
T *+39 06 487 3122*
W *www.trattoriamorgana.com*

TRATTORIA VECCHIA ROMA

The first time I climbed down into this basement-level room, a huge space with red and green walls opened up before me. Despite its size, the space was packed full and, despite being one of Rome's historic trattorias, it can feel for a second like you've wandered into a beer hall in Munich. This is a basement full of happy people who tend to hang out for a long time, some a little tipsy after a lot of red and white wine. You can come here in a large group – the more the merrier. In contrast, Italians say, "*Pochi ma buoni*" ("Few people but the right ones") – but that doesn't necessarily apply at Trattoria Vecchia Roma.

Travelers from Asia have found the place and in among all the Romans I see several groups of Japanese visitors. It's carefully organized chaos.

The menu is enormous with a long list of specialties. I look around; few are eating pizza, nearly everyone chooses pasta.

Many choose the house menu for 27 euro with antipasto, *amatriciana* and then oxtail or tripe, accompanied by fried potatoes or green veggies. The price also includes wine, mineral water, dessert and coffee.

The signature dish here is the house *bucatini all'amatriciana*. The waiter performs a magic trick in front of the guests – I watch skeptically at the way he pours a transparent alcohol (definitely not cognac) over the pasta and tomato sauce before lighting it on fire and tossing everything into a large hollowed-out rind of pecorino romano cheese. To my surprise, the pasta is actually good, despite the added spirits. The tomato sauce with smoked meat is well-made and the portion is generous.

If you're a lover of haute cuisine, don't come here! But the trattoria's many customers create a fun and vibrant atmosphere. In 2016, Vecchia Roma celebrated its 100th birthday; run by four generations of Tripodina family, it will surely last a few generations more. Book well ahead of time – as early as Monday if you want a table at a decent time for the weekend.

O *Open every day except Sunday*
A *Via Ferruccio 12B–C; Esquiline – near Via Merulana*
T *+39 06 446 7143*
W *www.trattoriavecchiaroma.it*

∧ **Oxtail** – *coda alla vaccinara*
❮ *Bucatini all'amatriciana* **is lit on fire before being served at Vecchia Roma**

A mural in Monti of Rome's Francesco Totti

IX A DAY IN MONTI

For many of Rome's visitors, Monti was a long overlooked neighborhood. Today the area I live in has become trendy. I don't know when it happened, but many of the neighborhood's craftspeople have slowly been replaced by small fashion boutiques, design stores and little bars and cafes. The neighborhood has become Rome's Village, the equivalent to London's Soho, although without the prominent art galleries.

The neighborhood is large and extends to the gate at San Giovanni. But the part that we're talking about mostly lies between the main streets of Via Cavour and Via Nazionale. Here there is a series of picturesque little cross-streets where time has stood still; Via degli Ibernesi ends in steep stairs and a little street fountain where a tired visitor can quench their thirst.

It's apparent that the neighborhood is ancient. Along the west side of Via Madonna dei Monti, if you head toward the Forum, you can see the antique columns from an ancient temple embedded in the walls. Rome's football fans have made their mark inside an old courtyard – a stylized graffiti painting of their beloved team captain Francesco Totti, who retired in 2017.

I always start my day at **Simon bar**, at Via di Santa Maria Maggiore 182–183, on the corner of Via Panisperna. Here Simona and Riccardo run one of the neighborhood's best breakfast bars, where foreign guests can have an international breakfast with eggs and bacon, toast and marmalade for 6 euro. I go here for the fresh *tramezzini* – triangular sandwiches with cheese and ham, or tuna and egg – and a cappuccino at the bar.

I also often go to the bar **La Licata** at Via dei Serpenti 165. A wider range of sandwiches, baked goods and pies is hard to find. *Cornetti salati* filled with prosciutto and just slightly grilled are excellent. The bar also sells tickets to Roma and Lazio's matches – everyone who wants to go to a match has to give their passports to the person buying the tickets.

The third place, **La Bottega del Caffè**, has a large outdoor seating area on Piazza Madonna dei Monti. It's a fairly trendy cafe that is open from 8am–2am, with excellent sandwiches and warm food. It has a hint of attitude – you can be denied a free table because they want to save it in case an important regular happens to come in. I don't mind. For me it's just a decent breakfast place where I can drink a perfect cappuccino and eat a good sandwich.

The neighborhood was free of tourists for a long time, maybe because there aren't really any major sights here. There is San Pietro in Vincoli – the church that has the chains in which the apostle Peter was supposedly locked up. The church is accessed through the steep staircase Salita dei Borgia. Visitors come to see Michelangelo's *Moses* that the artist did for Pope Julius II's tomb. But like so many of Michelangelo's works, it was never finished.

Monti means "the hills", and the neighborhood includes three of Rome's hills: Esquiline, Viminal and Quirinal. The main street, Via Panisperna, runs east to west, and its name refers to the fact that there were monasteries here that gave *panis et*

Piazza Madonna dei Monti

perna (bread and ham) to the neighborhood's poor.

The lower part of the neighborhood, after Suburra, slopes down toward the Colosseum. This was the area's lowest point and in ancient times it was just a big swamp.

Nightlife in Monti is intense and the bars for *aperitifs* are many. A nice place I feel quite at home at is **Er caffettiere**, at Via Urbana 72/73. Spartaco runs the place and has a plentiful all-you-can-eat buffet for 8 euro, including drinks. But the neighborhood doesn't lack eateries. In summertime, the pizzeria **Alle Carrette** has a large outdoor seating area; enter at Via della Madonna dei Monti 95. Via Urbana is still the main restaurant street, where there are many tourist traps. The safest choices are **Broccoletti** (p. 58) and **Sciuè Sciuè** (p. 95). Among wine bars, **Tre Scalini** at Via Panisperna has a great reputation. And don't miss the Sicilian bakery **Ciuri Ciuri's** cakes at Via Leonina 18–20.

The real nightlife happens at the square Piazza Madonna dei Monti, the heart of the neighborhood, where most people drink beer while standing or sitting around the square's fountain. Those who want to go to one of Rome's trendiest places can try **Black Market** at Via Panisperna 101. On weekends there are always lots of people, and several rooms to choose from, including a bar and dining room. In the largest room there's even a little balcony where couples can sit, drink and canoodle. There's a retro-feel here, but the age range is between 25 and 35. If you're any older, you're clearly

too old to be here, but you can still enjoy a whiskey and people watch.

Monti isn't really a "nice" neighborhood. Even in antiquity it was at a lower street level, *sub-urbe*, and therefore was called Suburra. Here there were sketchy taverns, both in terms of the food and the tart, sour wine that was served, and also the visitors who came here to drink their fill. Historians say Emperor Nero used to come here incognito to hear what people really thought of the city's rulers.

Monti was also home to many of Rome's bordellos, where Emperor Claudius' wife Messalina prostituted herself under a different name. On my own street this activity still happens, which I at first was totally unaware of when I moved in! The police don't intervene because prostitution isn't illegal in Italy.

These days the word *suburra* lives on and has given its name to a new TV series about crime and the Mafia. I sometimes wonder if people have any idea when they talk about "suburban" areas that the word suburb originated right here in my neighborhood just over 2000 years ago.

RESTAURANTS

Rome has many excellent and elegant eateries to choose from; the following selections are my personal favorites. The best ones have an enduring character and timeless ambiance. Some have very good prices, but the important thing is that the quality of the dishes is worth the cost. Some of the places are small and relatively simple, but the food differs radically from the city's classical trattorias.

ARCHIMEDE SANT'EUSTACHIO

Those looking for a good restaurant with a large outdoor seating area in the city center often look in vain. The food can be disappointing and instead you pay for the view – Piazza Navona isn't mentioned once in this book in relation to food. But Archimede is one happy exception, in this little square alongside the church Sant'Eustachio. Time seems to have stood still and the food is as good as it was two decades ago. A glance at the buffet by the entrance, with selections of vegetables and desserts, is enough. The restaurant is focussed on family tradition; Bruno Lucci, who started the place, is still occasionally here. Today his daughter Emanuela is in-charge, along with her husband Emilio.

The housemade egg pasta *tagliolini alla marina* with fish and shrimp is mild but flavored with fresh sweet tomatoes and a thin layer of frothy vegetable sauce at the bottom adds delicious creaminess to the dish. An unusual culinary combination, but the mixture is perfect. The prices here are good, like their grilled salmon with lemon sauce and zucchini marinated in mint for 14 euro. The menu is extensive. My favorite dish is their *melanzane alla Parmigiana*; this eggplant casserole with mozzarella is made fresh in the oven and takes 20 minutes; towering, generous and perfect for sharing between two. It's easy to get a table but if you want to secure a table outside, it's best to book ahead.

O *Open every day except Sunday evening*
A *Piazza dei Caprettari 63; Center – near Pantheon*
T *+39 06 686 1616*
W *www.archimedesanteustachio.it*

ARMANDO AL PANTHEON

It's been a long time since there was anything that was properly authentic on Piazza della Rotonda, as the square in front of the Pantheon is actually called. Tourists and school groups flock here. Waitstaff loudly beckon visitors into expensive and not particularly good restaurants.

In one corner of the square, behind a very anonymous entrance, lies the gem Armando. It's facade is unchanged since Armando Gargioli opened his little eatery in 1961. These days it's his sons, Claudio and Fabrizio, who cook the food; and with four grandchildren already, the future of this family-run restaurant seems to be more than secure.

The menu is just the right size with a balanced mix of Roman classics and other intriguing eye-catching dishes. Among these are *faraona* (guinea hen) with bolete mushrooms cooked in dark beer, and *anatra* (duck) in white wine with prunes. Ask about the day's specials. On Thursday they serve oxtail and on Tuesday *cernia* (filleted grouper) on a bed of potatoes with artichokes or chickory. The simplest dishes are often the best, like the house stew made of specially crafted *salsiccia* (sausage) and beans.

Finish your meal with one of their homemade desserts like *torta antica*, a cake with sheep-milk ricotta and strawberry jam. There's a good wine list that also includes several half-bottles, both red and white.

Book early, at least a week ahead for dinner, because it's always busy. Romans often improvise and decide to go out to eat at the last minute, which unfortunately has meant that foreign visitors have taken over. But the food remains the same. Views of the famed Pantheon is a major plus here.

Have an espresso outside after your dinner and enjoy!

- **O** *Open every day except Saturday night and Sunday*
- **A** *Salita De' Crescenzi 31; Center – adjacent to Pantheon*
- **T** *+39 06 688 03034*
- **W** *www.armandoalpantheon.it*

_____

L'ASINO D'ORO

The cook Lucio Sforza does everything right in this exclusive little neighborhood bistro with lofty ambitions. It's not easy to choose what to eat; most things on the menu are unusual. We started with a little omelet with chickory and divine ricotta. Their fresh pasta *lombrichelli* (literally "small earthworms") is genuinely handmade and served with goat cheese, chopped walnuts and wild chickory. Then I ate the housemade tongue, the most tender I have ever tasted, marinated in vinegar and cooked in red wine. It's served partially covered with a thick anchovy sauce that makes for a perfect flavor combination. My friend tried calf cheek that melted in the mouth and was served slightly warm covered in an egg yolk–tuna sauce.

There's still a lot to try on the next visit: *oca* (goose) served as a stew with cherry as a sweet contrast; the classic Tuscan meat stew *peposo* – the name indicates that the red wine sauce is sprinkled with black pepper. You can also have a classic bread soup from the same region.

For 10 euro you can choose a tasting menu with three of the house desserts. The tiramisu is made of bread instead of the classic *savoiardi* cookies. We chose a *vellutata di fondente* – chocolate cream flavored with coffee, shaved licorice and red chili. *Crema fredda* is a more solid construction of chocolate with almond macaroons and peppermint.

There are very few wines by the bottle, but there's a more extensive offering of wine by the carafe, both by the quart and the half-liter. It's a budget-friendly initiative, but a head-scratcher when you consider the high quality of the food here. At lunch a simpler menu is served. It includes a basic starter, soup, pasta and a main dish with extras like mineral water.

Ⓞ *Open every day except Sunday and Monday*
Ⓐ *Via del Boschetto 73; Center – Monti*
Ⓣ *+39 06 489 13832*
Ⓦ *www.facebook.com/asinodoro*

BROCCOLETTI

Via Urbana is the Monti neighborhood's boutique and restaurant street. Broccoletti is one of the street's smallest inhabitants and this little neighborhood locale gets full quickly. Despite a tiny kitchen, the owners Fabrizio and Giampiera offer up a surprisingly large menu that changes nearly every day. The stew with freshly cooked octopus pieces, tiny plum tomatoes, olives and oregano was perfect. The chili-spiced egg pasta is served with clams, while the house *amatriciana* comes with crispy pork and a splash of balsamic vinegar in the sauce.

Desserts are homemade, like for example the apple and ginger crumble. There's a long list of local wines available, all from the Roman region of Lazio.

Ⓞ *Open every day except Monday*
Ⓐ *Via Urbana 104; Center – Monti*
Ⓣ *+39 06 902 71389*
Ⓦ *www.facebook.com/broccoletti3102*

CAPO BOI

This genuinely elegant bistro in the Coppedè neighborhood serves food from Sardinia; its name comes from a well-known promontory on the south coast of the island. They almost exclusively serve excellent fish dishes. We started with the soup *fregola*, with tiny delicious pasta grains, shrimp and saffron. Then we had a massive spaghetti with *aragosta* (Mediterranean crayfish). It's worth trying the house fish *spigola* (sea bass) which is oven-baked under a salt crust. Ask to see the menu and remember that you pay for the freshest fish by size, so it's easy for the bill to inflate quickly, especially if you say yes to the waiter's generous starter suggestions, like lemon-marinated scampi, fish carpaccio and tuna tartare.

The ambiance here is a long way from a luxury restaurant. It is always full and quite noisy, with very little space between the tables, as if you were at a trattoria. It's best to avoid Friday and Saturday evenings. The best seating is in the cute little outdoor seating area.

Dining here gives you the the perfect opportunity to get acquainted with Sardinia's prestigious white wine vermentino from the province Gallura, where the chalky soil produces an unequaled flavor. It's a white wine that manages to be both dry and lightly fruity. Capichera is the most well-known vermentino producer, while Argiolas is considerably better priced.

Ⓞ *Open every day except Sunday*
Ⓐ *Via Arno 80; Trieste – near Viale Regina Margherita*
Ⓣ *+39 06 841 5535*
Ⓦ *www.capoboi.net*

CUOCO & CAMICIA

A clean and modern space, without being too cold and impersonal, Cuoco & Camicia is in the city centre, on a back street adjacent to the metro Cavour and the street Via Giovanni Lanza.

Chef Ricardo Loreni opened this place after graduating with honors from the bistro **Le Tre Zucche**. The menu is creative with interesting contrasting taste combinations. We ate egg pasta *fagottelli*, filled with lean pork from black pigs, served with chopped hazelnuts, apple and garnished with concentrated wine juice, *mosto cotto*. Their upside-down *carbonara al contrario* turned out to be black ravioli filled with egg and pork. The octopus stuffed with chopped boiled endive salad is a dish you will want to eat over and over again. The octopus comes sliced, but not all the way to the bottom, so that the filling stays inside. It's served with *guazzetto*, a reduced fish stock of mussels and clams, rich with the taste of saffron. For dessert there's a brûlée pudding placed on thinly sliced strawberries and ringed with balsamic vinegar. A tasting menu with six dishes costs 69 euro.

Points off, not for the wine list, but for the lack of wines available by the glass. A restaurant at this level should really have a good red and white wine selection to buy by the glass, but this bistro obviously wants to sell the whole wine package, which is unusual in Rome.

O *Open every day for dinner, also lunch Wednesday to Friday*
A *Via di Monte Polacco 2–4; Center – Monti – adjacent to Via Cavour*
T *+39 06 889 22987*
W *www.cuocoecamicia.it*

DA BUCATINO

The city's best *amatriciana* can be found almost anywhere – it's a dish that, truth be told, is difficult to get wrong. Here they serve it in a large bowl with a generous amount of pecorino. The dish's chubby, thick spaghetti tubes gave this restaurant its name. It is hard to even consider a main dish after this mountain of juicy pasta from the gods.

For those guests who come relatively early there's a large antipasti buffet to start with (although dishes run out very quickly), called *carretto delle svojature*. It's hard to translate; it means to fully indulge in all your temptations, where it is implied that the food is only the beginning. The name is a leftover from the restaurant's earliest owners, but the "new" regime has already been here for more than 35 years. They have kept the old traditions and made no changes to the premises, either.

The menu at Da Bucatino is extensive. There's a fish risotto, *oro*, a creamier version with *scampi* (shrimp)with a hint of tomato. I once tried the grilled octopus skewers, which were perfectly tender and bursting with flavor. The most simple dishes are often the best, like *pollo e peperoni* – Roman chicken stew with paprika and tomato. Everything here is seriously generous!

This is one of Rome's most food-happy bistros, which fills up every day with locals from the Testaccio neighborhood.

O *Open every day except Monday*
A *Via Luca della Robbia 84; Testaccio*
T *+39 06 574 6886*
W *www.dabucatino.it*

At Cólline Emiliane all the egg pasta is
made by hand each day (p. 62)

COLLINE EMILIANE

Emiliane is a decadent world of cream and butter, where you'll never care about counting calories. This little restaurant has been run by the same family since 1967, and it proudly offers up its regional comfort food. Book a table well in advance at this tiny space.

Those who walk by here in the morning and early afternoon can watch through the window as two women roll out their wafer-thin pasta. With nimble fingers they shape the dough into smaller pieces, and then, at a furious pace, they fold the pasta into tortellini and larger tortelloni, filled with ricotta and spinach or with pumpkin, crumbled almonds and a hint of mustard-marinated fruit – a variant from the city of Mantua. Tortelloni is generally served with just melted butter, sage and grated parmesan. Of course, there's also egg pasta, like tagliatelle, with a *ragù alla Bolognese* that might even tempt a vegetarian to make a meaty exception.

Probably the only dish that pleases the entire capital city is also served here, *passatelli*. This specialty homemade fresh pasta is made from egg, breadcrumbs and a lot of parmesan. The pasta is produced with the help of a potato press but with slightly larger holes. It only requires brief cooking before it's served up in a delicious chicken broth.

Among the starters on offer is a magnificent *culatello di Zibello* (Parma ham), made using the best cuts of pork, plus mortadella. Among the main dishes, try the *bollito misto* (boiled beef) with green sauce. Continue with fried meatballs and mashed potatoes or roast beef with fresh sweet-sour spring onions.

Save room for Paola Latini's homemade desserts: chocolate pudding, mousse of *zabaione* or caramelized pear tarte are some of her classics. And there's also her *meringata* (lemon meringue pie). After having this divine creation, an American regular once wrote in a thank-you note: "Before I die I hope I can come back here and enjoy Paola's meringue again. It alone is worth the trip to Rome". Those who wish to follow tradition should choose a flask of the region's red sparkling lambrusco wine; light and fresh with a lot of acid that balances out the food well.

O *Open every day except Sunday night and Monday*

A *Via degli Avignonesi 22; Center – near Via del Tritone*

T *+39 06 481 7538*

W *www.collineemiliane.com*

Classic tortellini filled with meat and the larger tortelloni filled with ricotta and spinach at Colline Emiliane

Strawberry tiramisu at Colline Emiliane

DA EDY

This place is a true find, located between the Spanish Steps and Piazza del Popolo – a neighborhood that's dominated by high-end fashion and design shops. This charming family restaurant (already into its third generation) lies on a little side street off Via del Babuino. It has a warm atmosphere and lighting – despite the brown tiles on the walls – that makes it feel like home as soon as you walk in. There's a large menu that includes both fish and meat. A sauté of clams turns out to be a whole mountain, with mussels. The foil-baked spaghetti, *al cartoccio*, with seafood was equally generous and delicious. Desserts are guaranteed to be homemade, including the enormous tiramisu served in a glass.

There are only a few tables outside. It's good value, especially if you consider the great quality and generous portions.

O *Open every day except Sunday*
A *Vicolo del Babuino 4; Center – near Piazza del Popolo*
T *+39 06 360 01738*
W *www.ristoranteedy.it*

FELICE

Felice has survived for 80 years and become a trendy modern bistro. For once, you won't leave feeling nostalgic over how the old tradition of trattorias have disappeared. Actor and director Roberto Benigni has remained a regular here. Felice Trivelloni, who started working with his father Guido, cooked food here for over 70 years. Today the place is run by his son Franco and the food heritage is intact, but a batch of new dishes have come along. The secret behind its success is the restaurant's first-class ingredients. Felice has had the same suppliers of meat, fish, vegetables, fruit and bread for decades – in fact well over 50 years.

There are many dishes, but the variety is carefully distributed over the seven days of the week. On Tuesdays and Fridays they serve fish: *frittura mista* (grilled fish), often with octopus and shrimp but sometimes *alla paranza* which means a whole fried fish – a dish that is on its way out because people have become spoiled and now want their fish served already filleted. The classic pasta dishes *gricia, amatriciana* and *carbonara* are served daily. The dish *tonnarelli cacio e pepe* has a special place on the menu; it's a pasta where the warm cooking liquid in the bottom of the pan is tossed together with shaved pecorino and sprinkled black pepper, and served by the waiter with a little show. Naturally Felice's spaghetti is still on the menu. The pasta is served with a sauce that cooks in a very short time and is made with small sweet tomatoes and fresh spices like basil, marjoram, mint, thyme and oregano. Instead of pecorino or parmesan, a layer of salted ricotta is grated over the dish. It's a must-try dish. Beef roulade and *saltimbocca alla Romana* are always on the menu too.

Then there are the daily specials: on Mondays it's *bollito misto*, different sorts of cooked meat with green sauce; on Tuesdays, soup of *pasta e fagioli* (brown beans); on Wednesday, rabbit and steak in red wine; on Thursday there's oxtail; and Friday means homemade egg pasta with mussels and grated pecorino. Saturday's specialty is *trippa* (tripe) in tomato sauce, and on Sunday they serve lasagne – it isn't a Roman specialty but is eaten all over Italy.

The whole menu is available on the website. You'll need to plan your visit to Felice and book your table a few days in advance. In the evening there are two sittings, at 7 and 9.30pm, and Romans usually arrive late.

The restaurant is modern with a new ceramic floor in the traditional style. There's not a lot of space between tables, just like in an old trattoria, and the noise level rises rapidly.

A big plus here is the wine list – a whole little book of wines listed geographically from north to south. Sadly it's only in Italian, but there's a competent sommelier on site – something that is very seldom found in a traditional trattoria.

- **O** *Open every day for lunch and dinner*
- **A** *Via Mastro Giorgio 29; Testaccio*
- **T** *+39 06 574 6800*
- **W** *www.feliceatestaccio.it*

DA ROBERTO E LORETTA

I can't hide the fact that I've been a regular here for a couple of decades. In the beginning, the place was on Via Gabi and was much smaller. The owner Roberto Mancinelli, who comes from Marche, runs the place with his wife Loretta and their son Riccardo who has been on the premises for a couple of decades. In 2005 they moved the restaurant to a larger location, but they've managed to preserve the familiar atmosphere. It's an intimate setting, with booths created with moving wall panels that divide up the space.

There's a large menu with many showpieces, and this is where you'll find the best bread in town! It comes to the table warm and is served with a fantastic fresh buffalo mozzarella with anchovies and truffle. Among the pasta dishes are an excellent thick *paccheri* (large tubular

Deboned lamb with artichoke at
Da Roberto e Loretta

Roberto Mancinelli

Loretta Mancinelli

pasta) with *spigola* (sea bass) in a thick tomato sauce with small olives called *taggiasche* from Liguria. The Roman bean soup *pasta e fagioli* appears here but as a unique seafood version with mussels and octopus. Otherwise, there's more meat than fish on the menu.

Even people who normally don't eat rabbit should try the deboned, truffle-packed *coniglio* that's served in slices. Their deboned lamb cooked with small artichokes that Loretta assembles in the kitchen is a must-try, ordered alongside the house potatoes, cut into millimeter-thin slices, as a side. They're fried and come as warm chips to the table – something that no other restaurant in all of Rome attempts to do.

Desserts are the restaurant's strongest selling point. Go for the house's sorbet *cremolato* made from strawberries; it tastes divine year-round.

The wine list is extensive. Choose a wine from the Marche region: white verdicchio or red from Monte Conero or Lacrima di Morro D'Alba – a good-value and flavorful, relatively light wine that has nothing to do with Alba in Piemonte.

Ⓞ *Open every day except Monday*
Ⓐ *Via Saturnia 18–24; San Giovanni – near Piazza Epiro*
Ⓣ *+39 06 772 01037*
Ⓦ *www.robertoeloretta.com*

DA ROMOLO ALLA MOLE ADRIANA

The area around the Vatican and St Peter's Basilica is the most difficult for finding quality restaurants. Don't go into the bars along Via della Conciliazione, they're mostly expensive and not good. One exception is this historic restaurant, which reopened again two years ago in a new modern and airy space. The majority of the customers are regulars, a list that includes people from the Vatican and the Pope's own circle. But as they say in Rome, "Where the priests eat, the food is good". That certainly applies here.

Fish dishes are generous and the vegetable side dishes are extremely fresh. As antipasti I ate a huge salad of potatoes and freshly cooked squid. The lukewarm squid was fresh enough to melt in your mouth – a perfect consistency that is rarely achieved. Classic Roman lunch dishes include the house soup with lentils or with

pasta and brown beans or chickpeas, and of course minestrone. This is not the place to eat pizza; there's so much else to enjoy.

Diners can glimpse part of the walls of *il passetto* – an elevated passage that was built so the pope could quickly leave the basilica and escape in safety to the well-fortified Castel Sant'Angelo nearby. The restaurant has a well-hidden outdoor terrace on the second level, which is the regulars' territory; ask in summertime about *la terrazza*, which is best to book beforehand. The street this restaurant is on is small and fairly unknown, but reachable from Borgo Sant'Angelo.

- **O** *Open every day except Monday*
- **A** *Vicolo del Campanile 12; Borgo – adjacent to St Peter's Basilica*
- **T** *+39 06 686 1603*
- **W** *www.daromoloallamoleadriana.it*

DA TEO

The pasta dishes here are an art form. Especially those with seafood, mussels and shrimp, served here under the Neapolitan name *allo scoglio*, where a few stray fresh tomatoes often sneak in. The best choice is the spaghetti with *aragosta* (Mediterranean crayfish) or *astice* (scampi). The dish isn't always on the menu, which is a good sign; it means the owner Teo only makes it when there are fresh ingredients.

Before your pasta dish, you should eat a Roman appetizer like fried artichoke or *puntarelle* – salad sprouts that are cleaned and put in water so they curl up; they are normally eaten with oil, anchovy and garlic. Teo also serves a *millefoglie*, thousand-layer cake, which alternates layers of Sardinian thin bread *pane carasau* and soft creamy burrata from Apulia. It's a sinful pleasure, which proves that Teo's

culinary skills go well beyond just the traditional Roman kitchen.

It's always packed here, so it's good to book in plenty of time, especially if you want one of the outdoor tables which have become even more scarce after local laws took effect; it's next to impossible to get one out on the little picturesque piazzetta. Even if you book you still might wait 45 minutes for a table. Those who book for 8pm and arrive early may be lucky.

For a long time Teo has run the place with Tiziana, who can often be both sour and unfriendly. Here you just have to compromise: ignore her attitude and just enjoy the food.

The place is best on a cold winter night; even then it will be packed-full with Romans, while all the tourist traps in Trastevere are desolate and empty.

- **O** *Open every day except Sunday*
- **A** *Piazza dei Ponziani 7; Trastevere – near Lungotevere Ripa and Ponte Palatino bridge*
- **T** *+39 06 581 8355*
- **W** *www.trattoriadateo.it*

DITIRAMBO

For the ancient Greeks, the word *ditirambo* was a cheerful tribute to fertility god Dionysus who was later associated almost exclusively with wine; it's an elegant name for this little bistro that has been here for a couple of decades. The menu changes a few times a year. Classics like *testaroli* – a unique, traditional pasta from Liguria that's first baked in a pan and then quickly cooked and served with pesto – return often to the menu. Oxtail comes with a puree of pumpkin and grated licorice.

A few years ago the kitchen started serving several creative vegetarian dishes like a radicchio gratin and pumpkin with smoked ricotta, vegetable balls of oven-baked eggplant with tomato sauce or fried crispy potatoes with cheese fondue and shaved truffle. As a starter there's the unusual pear souffle with gorgonzola and a hint of balsamic vinegar. This is not a fish restaurant, but there are two fish dishes on the menu. The only negative is that the tables are very tight, but you quickly forget that. I never leave here feeling anything but content.

O Open every day except Monday lunch
A Piazza della Cancelleria 74; Center – adjacent to Campo dei Fiori
T +39 06 687 1626
W www.ristoranteditirambo.it

_____

DUE LADRONI
The Piazza Nicosia, a square centrally located near the Tiber and the ancient Campo Marzio, contains one of the city's largest outdoor seating areas. The name Due Ladroni (the two thieves) has a long history – it came about after WWII, when two new owners took over the old trattoria and replaced it with a high-end restaurant with higher prices. Unhappy customers jokingly referred to the owners as the two thieves.

Today Due Ladroni is a major culinary destination in the city and a name that the owners aren't ashamed of in the least. The place isn't cheap, but the quality of the food is high and the service is perfect. Without hesitation I can guarantee this is a place where you'll find more seafood dishes than meat options to choose from. We ate a delicate bruschetta with clams and tomatoes, then tagliolini with shrimp and a hint of lemon and pecorino in the sauce. The oven-baked *spigola* (sea bass)

breaded with chopped pistachios and shaved ginger is a dish you'll remember for a long time. For those who don't care about the bill there are oysters or Catalan salad made of lobster, crayfish and shrimp for 36 euro.

Among the more unusual dishes is *risotto al salto*. It's the only place in Rome where I've seen this dish, strongly associated with Milan, on offer. The dish originated as a way of using up leftover risotto. Now the risotto is made expressly for this classic preparation method, *alla Milanese* – with butter, broth and saffron. When nearly all the liquid has been cooked off, but before the risotto is fully cooked, you let it simmer in a pan like an omelet. And soon you have a crispy, delicious risotto that's still buttery and soft on the inside.

Rome's city center has become more of an early evening zone – something that happened because many places adjusted their times to suit tourists. But this place doesn't open before 7.45pm and you can come in without a booking as late as 11.30pm to eat dinner in peace and quiet, hopefully beneath the city sky.

O Open every day except Saturday lunch and Sunday
A Piazza Nicosia 24; Center – Campo Marzio, near the Tiber
T +39 06 686 1013
W www.dueladroni.com

_____

FLAVIO AL VELAVEVODETTO
You can rightly say that this restaurant is ancient. On a glowing, warm summer night, those who have booked a table are eating out in the garden or on the quaint terrace – a section of small, secluded tables. Inside the dining room,

the temperature is perfect, thanks to the ancient air conditioning. Behind glass windows we see walls with ceramic tiles – a part of Monte dei Cocci, the pottery mound that grew over a few hundred years and became 115 feet (35 meters) high. It started in Emperor Augustus' time when people in the area adjacent to the harbor Emporium unloaded enormous amounts of goods. We are on an ancient garbage dump where around 53 million pottery jars, which were primarily filled with oil, have been left behind. The shards have been packed down over several hundred years. The air that comes from the walls is cold, enough so that the waiters have only one of three glass doors open just slightly and the whole room maintains a perfect temperature.

This rustic and fun restaurant is wholly focused on Roman food; large pasta dishes and oxtail with Rome's thickest tomato sauce – a delicacy. In Italy Wiener schnitzel is normally called *cotoletta alla Milanese*, but not in Rome. Here people speak only of *fettina panata*. It arrives as a breaded slice of beef as large as an elephant ear. The new owner Flavio di Maio has brought with him his pasta dish with fresh tomatoes, creamy ricotta and a variety of herbs from his previous workplace, **Felice** (p. 63). Now this delicious pasta dish exists at two of the city's restaurants. Here it's named after the restaurant, *spaghetti al velavevodetto*, a word that is best translated as "that's what I said". It's hard to know exactly what the name is alluding to – maybe that people eat well here?

The menu is relatively small and changes daily. The wine list, however, is enormous, with many exclusive wines, which attests to the fact that this is a hot spot. It looks a bit like a simple trattoria but it is considerably more expensive. You may be partially paying for the unique location, but it's worth it. The restaurant's most charming on a warm summer evening; book ahead to be sure you get a seat outside. Located just 10 minutes from the metro Piramide.

- **O** *Open every day for lunch and dinner*
- **A** *Via di Monte Testaccio 97; Testaccio*
- **T** *+39 06 574 4194*
- **W** *www.ristorantevelavevodetto.it*

GRAPPOLO D'ORO ZAMPANÒ

This restaurant has been around for a long time and it's possible Federico Fellini ate here. Its nickname, Zampanò, the main character in the film *La Strada* (played by Anthony Quinn), hints at this. Today the place is a totally modern and refurbished space. It's sufficiently charming, but is a good restaurant too, not least because it lies precisely adjacent to the touristy square Campo dei Fiori.

The house antipasti *misti* is generous, with meatballs and green sauce, Tuscan panzanella and creamy burrata with anchovies. The spaghetti *alla carbonara* stands among Rome's best, as does the house *amatriciana*. When it comes to the best main dishes it's a tie between *stinco alla birra* (pork shanks in beer) and *guancia* (beef cheeks) cooked for several hours in red wine. There's a good wine list, but even the house wine by the carafe is of a high standard.

- **O** *Open every day except Wednesday lunch*
- **A** *Piazza della Cancelleria 80; Center*
- **T** *+39 06 689 7080*
- **W** *www.hosteriagrappolodoro.it*

At Hostaria Romana Boccaccio
scribbling on the walls is allowed (p. 72)

Owner Ivano Camponeschi serves in the dining room at Hostaria Romana Boccaccio (p. 72)

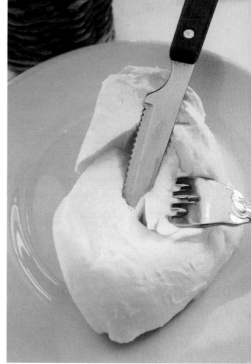

 HOSTARIA ROMANA BOCCACCIO

The large glassed-in veranda fills up for lunch in five minutes flat. Regular guests file in, among them are well-dressed people who are here to eat lunch and talk business. Those who haven't booked are guaranteed to be without a table, because this is one of the best addresses in the city center.

Begin with the house antipasti which is a substantial mix of salami, fresh ricotta, mozzarella, just-made omelet, mushrooms and perfectly grilled and marinated zucchini and eggplant. After this, try Rome's creamiest *carbonara* with several egg yolks and crispy, lean salt pork, which gives the classic dish an unexpected lift and character. The osso buco with mushrooms and peas comes next, perfect for a very satisfied guest who has the world to conquer.

This is a restaurant that inspires a real sense of joy about food; a bistro that encourages long relationships. Caricature drawings from the '50s still decorate the walls, a remnant from the previous owner Gigi Fazi. But the Camponeschi family, who took it over after Gigi, have already been here some 37 years.

In the lower dining room, guests are free to scribble on the walls and write greetings and reviews. The walls are repainted every three years.

O *Open every day except Sunday*
A *Via Boccaccio 1 x Via Rasella; Center – near Via del Tritone and Piazza Barberini*
T *+39 06 474 5284*
W *www.hostariaromana.it*

LA FIASCHETTA

La Fiaschetta is a newcomer to the neighborhood adjacent to Campo dei Fiori, where tourist traps lie in rows. Owner Giuliano Rossi has taken the long road here. He started with a wine bar and gradually expanded. For the past five years it has been a restaurant; a charming one, with rustic decor. The name is a tribute to the region's classic basket-encased wine bottles.

The food is a couple of notches above the classic trattoria and takes its inspiration from Tuscany. We had an unusual fettuccine with octopus, plum tomatoes

∧ Possibly Rome's best *carbonara*, thrown together at the table at Hostaria Romana Boccaccio (p. 72)
‹ Ultra fresh mozzarella among the antipasti dishes at Hostaria Romana Boccaccio (p. 72)

and *guanciale* (pork cheeks). Seriously good with grated pecorino on top. Grilled tuna and zucchini on skewers is a solid choice, or delicious fried lamb cutlets, or beef tenderloin in red wine sauce served with the city's best oven-baked potatoes. A sweet and creamy mild *crema catalana* with perfect burnt sugar rounds off the meal. There's a handwritten wine list, with the added bonus that the house uncorks many of the wines to serve by the glass.

O *Open every day except Monday*
A *Via dei Cappellari 64; Center*
T *+39 06 682 10599*

LA GENSOLA

One of Trastevere's best restaurants, La Gensola is relatively large, but the unusual hallways make the place feel intimate. The atmosphere tells you for sure that this is a family restaurant. The husband and wife team of Claudio and Irene Dordei took over in 2005 and have continued to develop the place. There are creative but at the same time simple fish dishes that take inspiration from southern Italy. Roulades of swordfish are served with *caponata* – a sweet and sour vegetable mix. Or quickly heated-up octopus with thinly sliced pork and capers which is another starter, as are the delicious scallops with pine nuts and fresh tomatoes. There are also simple, old-fashioned dishes like spaghetti with breadcrumbs, pine nuts and small raisins, flavored with *colatura di alici* (fish sauce) from the Amalfi coast – a modern variation of ancient *garum* (a fermented fish sauce).

Among the hot dishes there's filleted John Dory (St Peter's fish) that's served with salad from the island Pantelleria – onion, potato, capers and fresh tomatoes. Several times I've eaten *rana pescatrice alla cacciatore*, anglerfish in white wine sauce with puree of apple and rosemary. The oven-baked fish with a salt crust is made perfectly – a dish for two, just like the fish soup *pezzogna brodettata*.

Here there are also the traditional Roman pasta dishes and divine and delicious oxtail in a thick tomato sauce. Look for the day's specials on the blackboard.

O *Open every day for lunch and dinner*
A *Piazza della Gensola 15; Trastevere – near Piazza in Piscinula*
T *+39 06 583 32758*
W *www.osterialagensola.it*

X TRASTEVERE – ON THE OTHER SIDE OF THE TIBER

Paris has its Rive Gauche (Left Bank), Florence its Oltrarno (on the other side of the river Arno) while Rome has Trastevere, a name that evolved in the same way as Oltrarno. Here it refers to the neighborhood on the other side of the Tiber.

Trastevere is home to many tiny streets and picturesque alleys. On a Friday or Saturday evening it gets crowded quickly. And even if many today tend to classify Trastevere as fairly touristy, I don't quite share that view because the local Romans have never left this neighborhood. Many of the city's inhabitants still come a long way to eat a pizza or a plate of pasta in this quarter.

Surprisingly, there are still countless old, one-of-a-kind food shops, bakeries, charcuterie shops and butchers that are going strong in this neighborhood. Swing along Via Natale del Grande and they're lined up in rows.

The neighborhood is divided by Viale del Trastevere, where the new accordion trams wiggle along like green earthworms. Tram 8 still has a stop for the neighborhood's traditional folk festival La Festa de'Noantri – "The festival for those of us who live in the neighborhood", (implying that outsiders shouldn't bother) – because it is no longer possible to turn off the street. That's also why all the festival's market stands have vanished.

The area of Trastevere that lies adjacent to the Tiber and near Piazza in Piscinula is considerably more relaxed and more authentic than the area around the church Santa Maria. In this area near Piazza in Piscinula you'll also find some of the better restaurants. One is **La Gensola** (p. 73). History tells us that the name Gensola refers to the fact that jujube trees grew here in the 1400s; the fruit the trees produce is slightly bitter, but good to eat and is sometimes called Chinese dates. There's been an inn here since the end of the 1700s. Several Scandinavian artists made this area their regular hangout in the 1800s, including the Danish sculptor Bertel Thorvaldsen, who lived many years in Rome.

Roberto Polica runs the cheese store Antica Caciara (p. 164) in Trastevere

LA GREPPIA

After a show at Rome's magnificent auditorium, if you want to eat well, go to La Greppia.

About 10 years ago, Claudio Brioschi took over this elegant restaurant with its enormous menu. The house bruschetta turns out to be made with homemade pesto, buffalo mozzarella and salmon. We followed that with *moscardini affogati*, small octopus in a light, creamy tomato sauce. It is listed as a starter, but is bigger than a normal main dish. Polenta with *spuntature* (spare ribs) and tomato sauce or bolete mushrooms are obvious choices for winter. We chose *baccalà* as it's done in Vicenza. The fish is consistently good and is served in a creamy sauce with olive oil, egg and parsley – a highlight.

Pizza, here called *pinsa*, is also available. We rounded our meal off with *elisir di cioccolato*, the house chocolate cake.

And now an elegy for how the kitchen fries food: nothing seems greasy, but is perfectly crispy. Try the delicious fish balls of *ricciola* (a mackerel-like fish), with cheese and a slew of other homemade ingredients. As a starter I also recommend the minced-meat-filled, breaded and then fried *olive ascolane*. It's a specialty from the city Ascoli Piceno in the Marche region – painstaking to makc, so it's always factory-made and deep-frozen. La Greppia is probably the only place in all of Rome that makes its own. The bistro is easily reached by tram 8 from metro Flaminio.

O *Open every day except Saturday lunch*
A *Viale Tiziano 73; Flaminio – adjacent to Via Flaminia*
T *+39 06 323 3449 or +39 33 581 54609*
W *www.osterialagreppia.com*

L'ARCANGELO

Arcangelo – the archangel – is a fairly unusual name these days. Arcangelo Dandini is one of the city's cooks whose name and skills stand out. He runs his own race, unswayed by trends like minimalism, fusion or *apricena* – as an extended *aperitivo* is called these days.

Dandini is the fifth generation running the restaurant. The family came from the village Rocca Priora which is found in the Roman wine district of Castelli Romani. After spending several years in the industry, Dandini still has a lot of fun with his work. The three small model cars on every table attest to this. But first and foremost Dandini's quest is to look to and follow Rome's culinary traditions going all the way back to antiquity.

My ravioli with *cipollata* (a soft onion filling), was served with a personal

Arcangelo Dandini

variation on the fish sauce *garum*, here made of sardines, wine, vinegar, rosemary and garlic. All carefully measured by Arcangelo with the precision of a pharmacist, but that doesn't hinder him from then generously grating parmesan on top.

The dishes on the menu are relatively few and change regularly. The pigeon with mustard, lightly smoked with rosemary impressed me, as did sweetbreads served with fried escarole salad. For dessert we enjoyed a soft, creamy chocolate ganache garnished with preserved orange peel on a golden mirror–like saffron sauce. A tasting menu with five dishes costs 60 euro. The place is small, so book early. The restaurant lies in the central neighborhood Prati which many tourists skip.

O *Open every day except Saturday lunch and Sunday*
A *Via Giuseppe Gioacchino Belli 59; Prati – near Piazza Cavour*
T *+39 06 321 0992*
W *www.larcangelo.com*

LA ROSETTA

When you think of how many new tourist places have opened around the Pantheon, this is a safe and solid choice for those who want to eat fish in the city center. The owner Massimo Riccioli has Sicilian roots, but over the years has become rather Roman. His Sicilian-ness shows in the quality of his produce – of the oysters, of course, but also the fresh *ricci di mare* (sea urchins). They make a perfect starter along with a glass of sparkling wine. Another way to lead in to mealtime is to order what Massimo calls Italian tapas. We tried mussels gratin with pork and croutons and another dish with guacamole and shrimp.

The pasta dishes are excellent, not least the baby octopus done in a seriously black pasta sauce. The flavor is delicate and the octopus melts in your mouth. The house linguine with shellfilsh and mussels is a classic that is nearly always on the menu.

Despite being such an exclusive restaurant, they offer many different fish dishes at a set price. The house *dentice*, which belongs to the sea bream family, is served with fresh bolete mushrooms,

❮ An old-fashioned decor and a hint of English in the red-leather dining room at L'Arcangelo

potatoes and olives. In the Mediterranean these fish can weigh up to 20 pounds (10 kilos) and can become a little dry and dull. But not here.

No meat dishes are served, but there's a separate vegetarian menu. From among the desserts we ate the decadent and unusual bread cake with chocolate and hazelnuts covered with a layer of pumpkin sorbet; fresh and just sweet enough, with an aftertaste of spices.

The restaurant has changed for the better, first and foremost by becoming more casual and accessible. These days there's a simpler lunch menu for around 28 euro that includes a starter and a pasta or main dish. It's served between 12pm and 3pm. If you can get an outdoor table, life immediately feels a little sweeter.

P.S. Yes, I fell in love. It doesn't happen so often these days. Try the wine producer Coppo's chardonnay that's called Monteriolo. I've never had such an elegant chardonnay with an unending aftertaste, and from a region of Piemonte that is known for its red wines. It is, of course, not cheap.

- O *Open every day 12pm–11pm*
- A *Via della Rosetta 8–9; Center – adjacent to the Pantheon*
- T *+39 06 686 1002 or +39 33 577 53971*
- W *www.larosettaristorante.com*

LA ZANZARA

This bistro is the Prati neighborhood's trendy meeting place from early breakfasts through to late-night drinks. It is also a restaurant where you can easily ignore all the rules that apply to Italian mealtimes. If you're a larger party and only a few of you want to eat, the others can just have a glass of wine. Here there are no constraints – you can eat as much or as little as you like. Maybe have something small like mozzarella or Spanish anchovies from Cantabria with your wine, or a Spanish classic like *pan y tomate*. There's also Iberian ham, which competes with Italian prosciutto and classic mortadella with pistachios. Not to mention the goose liver and the cheese. Naturally there's also pasta and a large range of grilled meats, but also the classic bistro dishes like Caesar salad with grilled chicken or their croque madame – toasted bread with gruyere, cooked ham and two perfect whole fried eggs. My favorite for a light lunch!

La Zanzara, which means "the mosquito", has a whiff of a continental capital city far from the rest of Rome. It's also a good restaurant where you can show up totally jaded after having run the gauntlet through St Peter's Basilica and the Vatican museum. The place is best at lunch during spring and autumn when you can sit outside. Book in the evenings if you're a large group, because even though the place is large it is often full.

- O *Open every day 8am–2am*
- A *Via Crescenzio 84; Prati – near Piazza del Risorgimento*
- T *+39 06 683 92227*
- W *www.lazanzараroma.com*

LE MANI IN PASTA

The regulars here are always in high spirits; the staff set a fun tone. The name already gives an indication of the atmosphere – a bistro called "Hands in the dough" can take a few liberties. It's pasta dough in this case, because they don't serve pizza here. The place

wouldn't exist without its cook Iviano Piras, who comes from Sardinia. He is the guy working in constant view behind the large glass panel. He does nearly everything himself.

Excellent pasta dishes, especially those with fish and shellfish, are on the menu. A portion of the dishes have a Sardinian origin, like egg pasta with fish and *bottarga*, which is dried mullet roe, or *gnocchetti sardi* with broad beans, tomatoes and truffle. Portion sizes are enormous. Here you cannot manage two dishes. The *sauté misto* with shrimp, mussels and clam, is perfect for two to share.

This is not purely a seafood restaurant. You'll find few other places with equally good meat dishes. Try the fillet with green pepper sauce or *alla Rossini* with red wine and truffle, named after an Italian composer who spent a long time in Paris and was a serious gourmand.

The wine list suits any budget. I don't know another bistro that adds on as little for their wine as they do here, around 10–15 percent more than standard store prices. If you eat fish I recommend the Sardinian wine Vermentino di Gallura (Argiolas). It's dry and minerally but still a tad fruity.

The restaurant is small and can be noisy, depending on who the other customers are – no two evenings here are ever the same. It's not a place for those who want a calm, romantic dinner. The cellar is more relaxed, but I avoid it; it feels a little depressing to eat there.

O *Open every day except Monday*
A *Via dei Genovesi 37; Trastevere*
T *+39 06 581 6017*

MACCHERONI

This restaurant located in the tourist-heavy area between the Pantheon and Piazza Navona. In spite of that, it has maintained its style and a decent menu. Here the food is made before your eyes – if you sit indoors you can see how the

At Maccheroni you see everything the cooks do

cooks work behind the large glass window. Total transparency; there's nothing to hide here. It's a rare and appealing feature. I can only think of a couple of bistros in Rome that also feature an open kitchen.

Maccheroni also has a large and fine outdoor seating area that attracts many guests. The place was once a charcuterie shop, and in one of the dining rooms there are metal hooks intended for salami and large hams still on the walls.

On the menu, there are classic pasta dishes like *amatriciana*, *gricia* (*amatriciana* without tomato sauce) and *carbonara*. The house gnocchi with gorgonzola and pear is a dish you definitely should try. Summer pasta *alla checca* consists of mozzarella, tomatoes, sliced cheese, olive oil, salt and pepper and is a Roman classic that is served at room temperature, almost like a pasta salad.

Maccheroni's other major specialty is grilled meat: steak or sliced beef *tagliata* with arugula, which here is called *rughetta*, in Roman style. There's also saltimbocca and osso buco. This is first and foremost a great lunch place.

O *Open every day for lunch and dinner*
A *Piazza delle Coppelle 44; Center*
T *+39 06 683 07895*
W *www.ristorantemaccheroni.com*

MALEDETTI TOSCANI

This restaurant might be uber-Tuscan, but the exuberant, friendly cook Ciro del Pezzo is actually from Naples. Here they serve food that honors Tuscany but with a bit of a vibrant new energy.

We ate classic crostini with chicken livers, capers and sage and tried *panzanella*, the cold bread salad with onion and tomato. We felt blessed that it was served covered in creamy burrata from southern Italy. My pasta *pici* from Siena came with a ragu of beef cheeks that melted in the mouth; the dish had character and matched the boldest of the region's red wines well. Pork tenderloin with vin santo and figs is another immediate hit and is balanced by the chili-spiced broccolini. Totally stuffed, we couldn't manage a dessert other than the dry biscotti, *cantuccini*, to dip into the vin santo.

Also here is real Tuscan meat that's grilled to perfection: *fiorentina*, fillet or ribeye. The menu varies a lot, explains the cook, and for a Tuscan, Ciro cooks a lot of fish. A showpiece dish in summer is the *cacciucco* (fish soup) that comes from the harbor town Livorno. The wine list is Tuscan through and through, when it comes to both red and white. At lunch there's a simpler and very affordable menu. The restaurant is in the north of the neighborhood Prati near Piazzale Clodio, which is the end station for many bus lines.

O *Open every day except Saturday lunch*
A *Via Monte Pertica 45; Prati – near Piazzale Clodio*
T *+39 06 375 13860*

The dessert "It's not a Snickers" is a gastronomic scherzo – a lightly gilded truffle bar filled with chocolate cream, caramel and peanuts served at Matermatuta

Stefano Podera and Valentina Antonini run Matermatuta

MATERMATUTA

In ancient Rome, Mater Matuta was the goddess of dawn and she had her own temple. This is the poetic name that the owner Stefano Podera and chef Valentina Antonini chose for their innovative, elegant restaurant.

Fish dishes are at the center of their menu, but there are a couple of exciting meat dishes too. Those who like starters have several to choose from including oysters, shrimp, crayfish, tuna tartare and fish carpaccio. The place is light and modern with shades of white, cream and ivory; all the strong colors come from the food. Like the black half-moons I ate – thin egg pasta dyed black from *seppie* (cuttlefish) – with a butterfly-light filling of squid and shrimp with loads of flavor. The dish is served with giant red mussels and diced vine tomatoes. It's pretty as a picture. Also fun and vibrant is the gnocchi with clams, black truffle and fried arugula. The color symphony continues with fish roulade filled with asparagus that sits on a gold mirror-like sauce of saffron alongside couscous.

The dessert "It's not a Snickers" is, as the name implies, a gastronomic sonata. It arrives as a lightly gilded truffle bar filled with chocolate cream, caramel, peanuts and other secret ingredients. Stately, but too rich and "impossible to pair with a dessert wine", says the waiter very truthfully. Next time I'll try the lightly frozen mousse of pistachio with jellied orange peel, or the house crème brûlée with star anise and powdered licorice. This is a place you will absolutely want to come back to.

The wine list is large and exclusive. By the glass, there are many wine options to choose from, but ask the waiter for advice.

I got a just-opened vermentino from Gallura in Sardinia by the luxury brand Capichera for 7 euro!

- **O** *Open every day except Sunday*
- **A** *Via Milano 48; Center – adjacent to Via Nazionale*
- **T** *+39 06 482 3962*
- **W** *www.matermatuta.eu*

MATRICIANELLA

A classic for several decades on a little street near Via del Corso, this place is always full, with many Roman regulars. It is a little crowded and noisy, but this is a restaurant that doesn't give you a hard time, and one of the few good places that exist in the city center if you don't want to go to a trattoria.

The pasta dishes are of course a must, like *bucatini all'amatriciana* (these days sadly linked to the earthquake in its hometown of Amatrice) and of course *spaghetti cacio e pepe*. Roman *abbacchio* (lamb) made in a variety of ways is equally good whether fried whole or as thin, juicy grilled cutlets. The house meatballs with truffles and arugula is another specialty. There's a good selection of cheese that gets competition from the also-very-good traditional desserts: pear cooked in red wine or warm pie made according to an old Jewish recipe with chocolate, mild ricotta and Nutella drizzled over the top. Absolutely necessary to book well ahead.

- **O** *Open every day except Sunday*
- **A** *Via del Leone 4; Center – near Piazza Borghese*
- **T** *+39 06 683 2100*
- **W** *www.matricianella.it*

ORLANDO

The best Sicilian place in town, now at a new address next to the once super fashionable Via Veneto, where Anita Ekberg and Marcello Mastroianni made film history. Today Orlando is one of the few reasons to visit the neighborhood. That's because it is genuinely and solidly Sicilian, with many ingredients directly from Sicily. The food is elegantly prepared with a careful nod to *nouvelle cuisine*. It's hard to choose from the large menu.

The house *alici* (anchovies) – the Mediterranean's answer to sprats – is prepared in four different ways: marinated, fried, as a roulade and as fish balls. "Angelica's kiss" is a gastronomic play on the dish *pasta alla Norma*. It's made with eggplant slices that form the body of the roulade, which is then filled with a rich pomodoro-drenched spaghetti and salted shaved ricotta. Yes, here you're glad the portions aren't quite so big. *Busiate* is a macaroni that is served with tuna, swordfish and almond pesto. Also delicious is the grilled tuna with chopped pistachios from Bronte in Sicily. Save room for dessert, like *perfetto di pistacchio*. This green, slightly frozen pistachio parfait is seriously addictive.

There's a big wine list that stretches across Sicily. Lunch and dinner is served. It is relatively expensive.

O *Open every day except Sunday*
A *Via Sicilia 41; Ludovisi – near Via Vittorio Veneto*
T *+39 06 420 16102 or +39 33 711 84387*

OSTERIA DELL'ARCO

This endearing little restaurant is a completely female-run operation. Led by chef Cristina Iemmi and sommelier Nicoletta Baiani, in the kitchen there's Emanuela, while Valentina serves. Cristina is from Emilia, which in the food world is a quality guarantee. She offers an inventive national cuisine made up of what she thinks is the best of Italy from north to south.

As a starter I chose fresh ricotta from Sabine served with *alla scapece*, marinated zucchini in the Neapolitan style. Lightly dried tomatoes give extra character to the cheese, as does an olive oil with the flavor of Roman mint. From Rome comes the tubular spaghetti that here isn't called *bucatini* but rather *perciatelli*, which is just a smidge thicker. Instead of tomato sauce Cristina has chosen to serve the pasta with tomatoes *au gratin* and a crispy *guanciale* (cured pork cheek) from the village of Cori, five miles southeast of Rome. A simple dish that has made the place famous. As a main course I enjoyed deboned guinea hen, a light meat subtly spiced with rosemary and sage, covered in a sauce of sweet and very ripe wine grapes. For dessert we had the Tuscan cake *castagnaccio* that's made of chestnut flour and served with coffee mousse.

The place is rustic with a vaulted brick ceiling. Along one wall there's a whole bookshelf that shows off the resaurant's many wines. The downside: the tables are too close together in a tiny room that holds 35 guests. Best to book ahead.

O *Open every day except Saturday lunch and Sunday dinner*
A *Via Giacomo Pagliari 11; Salario – adjacent to Piazza Alessandria*
T *+39 06 854 8438*
W *www.osteriadellarco.net*

PAPAGIÒ

At the Colosseum tourist traps will soon occupy every street corner. But you don't need to wander particularly far along the side streets to find a whole other culinary world. At Via Capo d'Africa, the bistro Papagiò has had a significant rebirth. Ten years ago the husband-and-wife team of Gionni and Giovanna Rossi took over the place. Today it is one of Rome's best seafood restaurants, with a high charm factor, not least because of the outdoor serving area on this quiet street.

Seafood dishes are packed with oysters, lobster, sea urchins, shellfish and fish from the sea along the Adriatic coast. The place is known for its antipasti, like carpaccio of different sorts of fish or tuna tartare. The menu is large and yet there are also daily specials. Last time we went, there was a warm soup with beyond-fresh beans and soft baby octopus. After that, John Dory fish *alla Gaetana* in the oven, perfectly cooked in the tradition of the fishermen who created the dish in Gaeta, south of Rome – with capers, olives and plum tomatoes. Among the pasta dishes there's *tagliolini* with large shrimp and sea asparagus (also known as samphire), or the unusual-in-Rome pasta made in sheets *al cartoccio* (cooked in foil, in the oven) with fish, where all of the flavors are preserved thanks to the cooking method. A big plus is the well-composed wine list.

- **O** *Open every day for lunch and dinner*
- **A** *Via Capo D'Africa 26; Center – near the Colosseum*
- **T** *+39 06 700 9800*
- **W** *www.ristorantepapagio.it*

PECORINO

Alfredo Lucarini is synonymous with quality. His long cooking career started in Trastevere and then continued in the Testaccio neighborhood, right across from the old slaughterhouse. Alfredo, who owns Pecorino, effectively provides diners with a cheat sheet to the best of the Roman kitchen. His classic pasta dishes shine, but the meat dishes may even be better: roulade, *saltimbocca alla Romana* and my favorite, *coda alla vaccinara* (Roman oxtail stew). Many restaurateurs make it with veal or heifer meat, but then there isn't much to eat. It's not every place that has the time or patience to let the dish cook for a sufficiently long time. It must simmer at least five hours, and is even better if left for six or seven hours, covered and carefully monitored. At Pecorino all the meat falls from the bones so easily you can pick it apart with a fork. The tomato sauce is perfectly thick with a hint of fresh celery. Here the cook and I share the opinion that there should not be any shaved chocolate in the sauce – one of Rome's big gastronomic traditions – because chocolate detracts from the fresh taste of the tomato and celery.

A couple of seafood dishes are always on the menu. Always ask, because it depends entirely on the fresh catch of the day. The place is large, but if you want to sit outdoors in summer it's best to book ahead.

O *Open every day except Monday*
A *Via Galvani 64, Testaccio*
T *+39 06 572 50539*
W *www.ristorantepecorino.it*

PERILLI

This is the type of mysterious restaurant where you never quite know what to do – go in or not? This historic place, which has always stood in the Testaccio quarter not far from the Cestius pyramid, has no menu posted outside. The irregular glass in the doors doesn't let you catch even a glimpse of anything inside. If you do go in, you enter the large dining room, the only room, with oak veneer on the walls

No menu outside? Take courage and step in!

covered with slightly kitschy paintings. It's a heavily traditional place, but always full and almost exclusively with Italians. Maybe this is why it doesn't need to show off or even have a website.

We ate a fantastic pasta with fresh artichoke. The house dish of well-cooked rabbit with herbs and white wine was impressive in its simplicity. Same with the succulent breaded and fried lamb cutlets, and the zucchini stuffed with ground beef – one of my favorite dishes that has become hard to find. Something else I recommend is the *pomodoro al riso* (rice-stuffed tomatoes). It's a dish that is only made in summer when the tomatoes are sweet and sun-ripe. At Perilli the menu reflects seasonal changes and ingredients. Ask the waiter for recommendations. There's a modest wine list.

O *Open every day except Wednesday*
A *Via Marmorata 39; Testaccio*
T *+39 06 575 5100*

PESCI FRITTI
This place could almost be a Greek tavern; everything here is done in light blue and white. It feels cozy and exotic. The menu is 100 percent Italian and exclusively seafood. Here you can go from the safely traditional, like a big plate of fried fish, shrimp, scampi and calamari, to the more adventurous, like *spaghetti carbonara* with fish instead of pork. The pasta with *amatriciana* sauce served with diced swordfish and grated pecorino is similarly surprising. Bruschetta with stewed octopus makes for a more obvious starter.

Good prices, but you probably shouldn't choose the spaghetti with lobster because when you consider the cost, it must have been frozen. Ask instead about

the day's fresh fish and see if they'll cook it in the oven with potatoes. All guests get good dry biscotti to dip in the house dessert wine.

There's a simpler lunch menu. A few tables outside in summer. The only drawback is the wine list. It has a fair selection, but the wines are not of a sufficiently high quality.

O *Open every day except Monday and lunch on Tuesday*
A *Via di Grotta Pinta 8; Center – near Campo dei Fiori*
T *+39 06 688 06170*
W *www.pescifritti.it*

POMMIDORO
In the student quarter of San Lorenzo I passed by Piazza dei Sanniti. Outside the restaurant Pommidoro – "tomato" in the Roman dialect – sat the 83-year-old owner, Aldo Bravi. I hadn't seen him for 10 years. He didn't recognize me, which wasn't unexpected, but even so he said, in a friendly manner, "Won't you have something to eat?" I stepped in. The restaurant had suffered a heavy loss in the years that had passed. Aldo's wife, Anna Desideri, who cooked food here for more than a half-century, is gone. But her recipes and cooking techniques still flourish. Their three daughters now manage the food and Aldo serves it.

As soon as I'd eaten the risotto with fresh bolete mushrooms and cream, I had an urgent question. "Where have you been all these years?" I said it, almost to myself. Masses of fresh mushrooms, perfectly cooked carnaroli rice and parsley; the best risotto I have ever eaten! This is one of the few restaurants in Rome that has game on the menu. The offering is mostly what

Aldo Bravi has hunted his whole life – primarily fowl. Snipe, or woodcock, as well as partridges are on the menu and roasted in the oven. As is wild boar, of course.

The place is elegant in an old-fashioned way. The menu is extensive and includes everything from ordinary beef dishes to the day's fish and a large selection of perfectly prepared vegetables. I ate roasted sweetbreads in white wine with a serving of chickory dressed in garlic and oil.

The dessert *zuppa Inglese*, common in Emilia, is perfect. It's made of a sugar-cookie crust drenched in the red liqueur Alkermes. Along the bottom is alternating layers of vanilla cream and cocoa and on top Pommidoro adds a layer of chocolate cream as an extra.

The restaurant is also known for the fact that **Pier Paolo Pasolini** (p. 132) ate his last meal here before going out into the Roman night, never to return. If you ask, Aldo will usually show you the check that Pasolini wrote, which he never cashed but instead had framed. Sadly Aldo doesn't leave it on display, for obvious reasons.

O *Open every day except Sunday*
A *Piazza dei Sanniti 46; San Lorenzo*
T *+39 06 445 2692*

 PIANOSTRADA

This is the most exciting restaurant in Rome in a long time. And it is definitely not a flash in the pan. We have seen this type of decor before, with small tables and mismatched chairs. But here they're interspersed with low and high armchairs. No table is like any other. Rarely has such cutting-edge decor been this cozy. In one corner there's an ornate wooden bar with a gleaming mirror. There is also a very popular inner courtyard to dine in.

The culinary journey began some years ago, selling simple street food in Trastevere. The overwhelming response from customers meant that the family who owned the place sought out a larger location on the other side of the Tiber which naturally had to be at street level – which is what the name Pianostrada means. The current location opened in November 2016. Mamma Paola Colucci and daughter Alice are in the kitchen, while sister Flaminia is responsible for the dining room and the cash register. Before this, no one in the family had any previous experience in the restaurant business.

The food is a mixture of the best dishes you can get in Italy. Pianostrada defines itself as a chef's laboratory, but the dishes seem logical and never contrived. All the bread is baked here, which is why the house *panini* are pure works of art – such as the freshly baked focaccia filled with figs and sun-dried tomatoes from southern Italy. As a starter we ate a delicious vegetable tempura with two sauces: one of beets and one of mayonnaise with finely ground almonds. Don't skip the day's pasta, they are the best dishes in the place. I can't possibly decide whether to my fresh egg-pasta with *guanciale* (crispy pork cheeks), fresh figs, lemon-scented thyme and grated pecorino was best or if my guest made a better choice with the *linguine Mancini* (a famous pasta factory from Marche) with diced swordfish, zucchini blossoms, small Taggiasca olives from Liguria, saffron, shaved ricotta and shaved organic lemon peel.

Certain ingredients make frequent appearances in dishes, like anchovies, lemon peel and the creamy soft cheeses burrata and stracciatella from Andria in Apulia. This is a restaurant you'll want to visit many times.

Roberto Lisi

If you are dining alone my tip is that you sit at the chef's counter and watch how the food is made. With this view you'll want to taste nearly everything. There are, of course, main courses, vegetable side dishes and dessert. The wine list is long, and there are good wines to order by the glass. Book with plenty of time, especially for the weekend!

O *Open every day except Monday*
A *Via delle Zoccolette 22; Center*
T *+39 06 895 72296*

PIERLUIGI

Some people sometimes try to imply that Pierluigi is a tourist trap. It's a sentiment I have never agreed with. This is one of Rome's most famous seafood restaurants. It has been in constant flux and development throughout the 35 years Roberto Lisi has run the bistro, which had a very modest start at the end of the 1930s. Today Roberto is joined by his son Lorenzo. There are usually many foreign visitors here, the cream of the crop who come to enjoy the restaurant's unique fish dishes. On top of that, Pierluigi happens to have the city's largest outdoor serving area on one of Rome's most beautiful car-free squares.

This bistro has never concerned itself with trying to be trendy or hip, but has instead devoted itself completely to quality. The Romans will never abandon this place. Take a look at the packed fish counter in the entrance. Inside is the restaurant's new cocktail bar, where bartender Vincenzo Tropea makes quality drinks and where you can order a few

dishes from the menu. If you choose the fresh fish, which is paid for by weight, the bill can easily blow out. My advice is that those who don't have unlimited credit on their credit cards shouldn't order the dishes that don't list a set price.

The best strategy here is to settle in and have an antipasti – their *moscardini* (small fried octopus) with pressed lemon is delicious – and after that a pasta dish, in order to avoid getting a disapproving look. It's almost a shame not to try their Catalan salad, where huge fresh shrimp is quickly tossed in a pan and then served with warm sliced potatoes, arugula, tomatoes and fresh red onion. Their mix of fish tartare is a beautiful symphony of colour – a dish that may get eaten up before you even have a chance to snap an Instagram-worthy photo to make your friends and family jealous.

There have been many new additions since my last visit. The house *amatriciana di mare* with crispy smoked pork and clams is a massive hit. Three or four meat dishes are also on the menu and they are definitely not just filler. Don't let it scare you off that the place can seat and feed 150 people; it doesn't feel too large, and the waiters here are never stressed. They take your order and serve your food with warmth and personality. Oaf that I am, I went to the restroom after eating and didn't think about how I left the table. When I came back my napkin was neatly folded. This happened twice!

Ⓞ *Open every day except Monday*
Ⓐ *Piazza dei Ricci 144; Center – square alongside Via di Monserrato*
Ⓣ *+39 06 686 8717 or +39 06 686 1302*
Ⓦ *www.pierluigi.it*

PINSA E BUOI

Few places are more excited about food in Rome than Pinsa e Buoi. You notice this as soon as you enter the rustic location, where cheeses are encased behind the counter along with a row of charcuterie. On the floor next to this is the Berkel meat slicer, a machine that has attained cult-like status in Italian homes. With surgical precision it slices the wafer-thin Parma ham and Roman salami.

The menu is like a Bible, with ten full pages – not including the wine list, desserts and the daily special that's written on the blackboard. This place requires strategy and planning. If you're in a large group, you can begin by sharing two charcuterie plates. Otherwise my advice is to start with some of the small appetizers, many of which are vegetable-based, like a strudel in paper-thin phyllo or vegetable casserole of buffalo mozzarella and white eggplant. A puree of broad beans with chickory and crostini is another unusual dish worth trying. After that, have a main course. The word *buoi* means oxen in Italian and it's clear that this is one place with more meat than fish. Try the *stinco* (pork shank) with potatoes or whole-fried and sliced beef *tagliata* which is served with bolete mushrooms or green pepper. It's good to save room for dessert, like lightly frozen creamy cheese with pistachio.

The wonderful pasta dishes, many served with black truffle in the fall, might have to saved for your next visit. There's also the house pizza, here called *pinsa*. The name comes from the fact that they roll the pizza out by hand. The pizza is long, rectangular, perfectly baked and comes in 46 different varieties! If you choose *pinsa* you won't be able to manage to eat much more, and that seems a bit of a shame at such a food-happy place. *Pinsa* is served only at dinner.

Note: there are two restaurants on the webpage with the same name and menu. Check that you're booking at the right place! The restaurant on Scalo San Lorenzo is best, mostly because the location is more personal and cozy. Tram 5 or 14 from Roma Termini to Porta Maggiore takes you here. The square is large! You'll reach Pinsa e Buoi in two minutes. The place is immediately to the left, after you have passed under the railway bridge.

(O) *Open every day for lunch and dinner*
(A) *Viale dello Scalo San Lorenzo 15–17;*
   San Lorenzo – alongside Porta Maggiore
(T) *+39 06 445 6640*
(W) *www.pinsaebuoiristorante.com*

RISTOCHICCO

Restaurateur Roberto Vaccini has moved to a new central location. It is hard to find a prettier cellar vault in Rome than this one from the 1400s that's inside Palazzo Taverna. Here the portions are enormous, so order cautiously! This applies particularly to the charcuterie or cheese plates that many diners start with. One plate is for two people according to the restaurant, but is easily enough for four. Order the house's warm, freshly made focaccia bread to accompany it. If you like the bread enough you can buy one to take home with you in the new little shop area near the entrance.

The pasta dishes are generous, especially the shellfish pasta *allo scoglio*. My favorite for a long time has been the house fish stew, *er barcarolo*, with whole fish. Skip it if you like to sit and relax

while you eat, because this dish is an epic undertaking, with both whole shrimp and mussels. The *grigliata mista* (mixed-grill meat plate) easily satisfies two. Again, make sure to have a plan – most stomachs have a hard time managing both pasta and a main course here. And don't be afraid to ask, because some of the dishes are normal-size, like *saltimbocca alla Romana*, where the whole pan comes to the table. I have never managed to eat a dessert here, but often finish things off with a little vegetable plate.

The son, Alessandro, is a competent sommelier and has put his soul into the large wine list that includes 250 labels. In the cellar's lower floor is a special room for up to seven people, perfect for wine tasting before you begin to eat.

(O) *Open every day except Monday*
(A) *Via di Panico 83; Center – near Via dei*
   Banchi Nuovi
(T) *+ 39 06 688 92321*
(W) *www.ristochicco.it*

ROCCO

Rocco is a welcome step back to Rome's more traditional restaurant scene. This is a newly opened, simple, but at the same time refined, neighborhood restaurant. The menu is written on the wall and is not huge. The pasta dishes are classic, like *amatriciana* and Neapolitan pasta *alla puttanesca*, which is fairly unusual in Rome; it's a dish that according to legend came into being when a street girl would quickly throw together a pasta for a hungry customer and take home what was left over: a few tomatoes, garlic, anchovies, olives and capers.

The menu also has Naples' special, thick soup made of pasta and potatoes. The *le polpette* (meatballs) are served with pressed

The chef Leonardo Palmieri at Rocco

lemon and made of *lesso* (boiled) beef and are fried until they're crispy on the outside. A must is the house lamb, which first sits for a long time in broth and then is dressed with whipped egg and herbs for a fricassée. A perfect apple cake with vanilla ice-cream finishes the evening. There's a good, if not very large, wine list: four reds and four whites that are available by the glass.

Naturally this place is family owned, by the siblings Sara, Lorenzo and Claudio Caligiuri. In the kitchen is Leonardo Palmieri, owner of the city's most stylish black beard. The little place gives an authentic and immediate sense of coziness. Rocco is a much-needed newcomer we've long been waiting for in the inner Monti neighborhood.

O *Open every day except Sunday dinner and Monday*
A *Via Giovanni Lanza 93; Esquiline – Monti*
T *+39 06 487 0942*

SAID

Anyone who logically expects, given the Arabic name, a place with a menu of Middle Eastern specialties is in for a real surprise. The name is an abbreviation of "The Italian limited partnership for candy". Out of the blue you're standing in an old chocolate factory founded in 1923, where as much of the original character has been preserved.

The family who owns the place still makes chocolate, pralines and caramel. Siblings Carla and Aldo De Mauro are third-generation and manage the candy tradition well. On the walls, the gleaming old chocolate forms are still hanging. The machine that once made mint pastilles is still set up, as is another that made and wrapped soft butter-caramels. A large metal table is the eatery's most popular space for a large group. Not everyone notices that the thick metal slab has a space that you can fill with cold water; the table was used to let the hot caramel solidify so that it could be cut when it reached the right temperature.

SAID functions as a retail store plus a bar, and many of its visitors arrive when it's time for *aperitivo*. But it's also possible to book dinner with an exciting variety of menu items. A few of the dishes on the menu have connections to chocolate. The house tagliatelle is rich with cocoa through the pasta dough; it's served with stewed rabbit and a hint of shaved chocolate. Steak tartare is carefully sprinkled with invisible chocolate microcrystals. Even the Sicilian warm sweet-and-sour vegetable mix caponata gets a few splashes of chocolate as a garnish. This creative and fun menu includes other dishes like ravioli filled with buffalo ricotta and fresh tomatoes. There are also many interesting vegetarian dishes; balls of pumpkin, potatoes and fresh ginger are served in a sauce of smoked provolone cheese from the region Campania. Chocolate definitely doesn't belong in an Italian summer, so this is a place to visit from early autumn until late spring. On a Sunday afternoon in winter it's full of Romans who come to drink hot chocolate with whipped cream, even if it's 60 degrees Fahrenheit (15 degrees Celsius) outside.

O *Open every day 10am–12am, except Sunday during summer*
A *Via Tiburtina 135; San Lorenzo*
T *+39 06 446 9204*
W *www.said.it*

___

∨ **SAID is an old chocolate factory in the San Lorenzo neighborhood with a uniquely authentic milieu**

SCIUÈ SCIUÈ

Rome is not overcrowded with Neapolitan restaurants. This is one of the simplest and best. The owners come from Naples and have run this consistently excellent little place for seven years. But only a few of the dishes here are Neapolitan, like the pasta *alla puttanesca* or the speedy dish *sciuè sciuè* (which means it's made quickly) – here it's a summer pasta with vine-ripe tomatoes and fresh basil.

The place is one of Rome's best when it comes to quality and affordability. Starters like an ample *frittura* with *moscardini* (small octopus) or oven-gratined zucchini flowers filled with shrimp, dried tomatoes and provalone earn high points. There's also an unusual risotto with gorgonzola and grated orange peel, an obvious culinary achievement from the first bite. *Lombrichelli*, fresh local pasta without egg, is served with calamari, fried *friggitelli* (mild green peppers) and soft grated sheep's cheese from Pienza in Tuscany. A warm dish of crispy grilled octopus on a bed of thick green sauce made of zucchini with sesame seeds is guaranteed to make you happy, as is the pork fillet with black pepper, cheese and fried bacon. Desserts are still Neapolitan: *pastiera Neopoletana* and chocolate cake with walnuts from Capri.

There's a good and affordable wine list with three whites and three reds available by the glass. Odds are you'll be delighted enough to return as soon as possible and try other dishes.

O *Open every day except Sunday*
A *Via Urbana 56–57; Monti*
T *+39 06 489 06038*
W *www.sciuesciueroma.it*

TEMPIO DI ISIDE

Probably Rome's most exclusive seafood tavern. And by that I mean a real tavern, not one of those fake, stylized luxury restaurants that you see sometimes on and around Via Veneto.

The luxury here is all in the quality and the ultra fresh fish. The Tripodi family took over the place in 1999 – before that it was just a simple fish trattoria – and it's Francesco Tripodi who each morning goes out to the fish auctions in Fiumicino, right by the sea where the boats come in with their haul. Only the best is good enough.

Many come here to eat the house's fish antipasti; giant barrels with super fresh, lightly marinated, peeled sea-crayfish, tuna tartare, carpaccio of giant shrimp and oysters. At the entrance there are two large aquariums full of live lobsters that can be cooked to order. The simplest dishes like pasta with mussels and sea urchins are an absolute highlight, as is the house fish risotto with shrimp and cheese. Thinly sliced, perfectly fried octopus is a warm starter. It arrives looking like golden moonbeams mixed together with thinly sliced, fried zucchini.

There's a large wine list with many top choices including Champagne and the best French white wines, on top of a large Italian offering. A visit here can be pricey, so if you don't have a platinum credit card it's best to study the menu and choose dishes that have a set price. But all of the finest shellfish, shrimp and fish are priced by weight.

The only thing I'm not totally sold on here is the atmosphere inside. It's elegant without being extremely showy, but the large space over two floors feels a bit impersonal and a long way from a warm family vibe. Book a table outdoors if it's a fine summer evening.

🄾 *Open every day except Sunday*
🄰 *Via Pietro Verri 11; Center – near the*
   Colosseum and along Via Labicana
🅃 *+39 06 700 4741*
🅆 *www.isideristorante.it*

TRATTORIA DEL PESCE

Modern and simple, without being minimalist – the single, majestic long table shines like a sun in the center of this restaurant. The place calls itself a trattoria but is an elegant seafood restaurant. The waiters come to the table with a giant barrel of the day's catch and all you have to do is choose. The ingredients come from the fish market in Porto Santo Stefano north of Rome. The young business owner Federico Circiello from Apulia opened this place five years ago after a career as a sommelier and maître d' at well known hotels in London and Rome. Some of the restaurant's cooks have come from Sicily and the Amalfi Coast and have left traces of southern Italy in the food.

A tartare of chopped tuna with beet greens is an elegant dish, flavored with orange and mint. The *Parmigiana* (eggplant casserole) made with the tiny glimmering silver spatola fish (also called bluefish) are delicate, light and perfectly baked with tomato sauce. The house *tagliolini* with bright-red shrimp, garlic and chili wins you over also. The pasta is decorated with chopped walnut, almonds and fennel seeds.

I get really thrilled when I find the rare fish soup *brodetto* from the Marche countryside on a menu. The dish's name means "a little broth", which of course is an understatement. It arrives as a giant platter with various little fish perfect for a soup, along with shrimp, crayfish, mussels and clams. It's a dish you can busy yourself with for a long time, because all of the ingredients are whole; it's like a seafood fountain flavored with fresh tomatoes, olive oil and a hint of garlic.

My tablemates managed a dessert of frozen pistachio pudding. The color, light pea-green, is natural and far from the mint-green shades you see in many commercial ice-cream shops. Here the pistachios certainly come from Sicily or Iran. The dessert is homemade, as are all the other desserts in the restaurant. There's a well-curated wine list that even includes some French wines, which one expects from a sommelier with international experience. In the Portuense neighborhood, bus 44 from Via del Teatro di Marcello to bus stop Val Tellina/ Duchessa di Galliera.

🄾 *Open every day except Monday lunch*
🄰 *Via Folco Portinari 27; Portuense near*
   Circonvallazione Gianicolense
🅃 *+39 06 959 45393 or +39 34 933 52560*
🅆 *www.trattoriadelpesce.it*

XI MEETING PLACE: THE PANTHEON

The Pantheon, whose proper name is Piazza della Rotonda, is Rome's most important square. It has always been a bit of a ritual for me to pass by here and grab a morning espresso at the counter of the bar **Di Rienzo**. Many have tried to copy this ancient temple, but there can only be one Pantheon.

The military commander Marcus Agrippa, who was married to emperor Augustus' daughter Julia, initiated its construction in 27 BC. The 16 granite columns most likely come from Sardinia or Egypt. Each column is 5 feet (1.6 meters) wide, weighs 60 tons and is carved from one piece. The cupola is very special because it has a 30-foot-wide (9-meter-wide) hole in the middle. An unknown builder created it from ancient cement – a stone filling that becomes lighter the higher up in the cupola it goes. After 2,000 years this unique cupola still rises high into the Roman sky. From a distance it looks super modern, like a flying saucer or UFO. The thing about the Pantheon is that we would not be able to construct such a building today. How's that for progress? On Pentecost the fire brigade climbs up on the roof and casts down thousands of red rose petals through the hole in the roof: a way of symbolizing the pentecostal miracle with the Holy Spirit in attendance.

PIZZERIAS

ANTICA STABIA

Without a doubt Rome's most authentic pizzeria for those who want to eat a real Neapolitan pizza. Behind the counter stands Raffaele Suarato, who 20 years ago left his hometown Castellammare di Stabia south of Naples for the capital. He started making pizza with his grandfather when he was just 8 years old, and has continued on for more than half a century.

The place is tiny – it's best to book a table – and an odd combination of Alpine hunting cottage and western saloon. The pizza is totally traditional with proper ingredients like buffalo mozzarella and local anchovies – Italy's best fom Raffaele's home district in the fishing village of Cetara. Naturally there's the classic Margherita, *diavola* (spicy) and calzones. The major discovery is the yellow tomatoes – mild and flavorful – I've never eaten the likes of them before. "They're called *spugnillo* and they come from Nola", Raffaele explained. "You know, the place where emperor Augustus died 2000 years ago!"

As usual it all comes down to the dough. Sixteen hours of rising does the trick, the maestro Raffaele says, emphasizing how important it is that the dough has a low moisture content, otherwise the pizza becomes gummy. The pizza comes out perfectly, without the tiniest bubble, so that you might think it was made in an electric oven, but from the table you can see the flames in the wood-fired oven. Here every pizza is like a newborn baby – watched with the utmost care.

Skip the beer and try the local red wine from Gragnano. It's sparkling and bold, but absolutely not sweet. Served well-chilled, it's perfect with pizza. A pilgrimage to the suburbs! Ten minutes' walk from the metro Monte Tiburtini or bus 163 from metro Rebibbia to bus stop Tiburtina/Bargellini, which is very close.

O *Open every evening except Monday*
A *Via Tiburtina 613; Tiburtino*
T *+ 39 06 439 8610 or +39 33 056 9890*

AL BIONDO TEVERE

Below the large outdoor terrace, the river passes by, strong and constant: the blonde, as it's called (because of its yellowish water), Tiber, which has been talked about since antiquity. It is nice to sit here on a warm summer evening. The place is authentic and tourists are few.

For over a hundred years this was countryside, although the mighty Basilica San Paolo *fuori le mura* (outside the city walls) lay very close. This building was a hay barn that was made into a *fraschetta* (wine store) in the early 1900s. Now for many generations it has been a restaurant and pizzeria. The pasta and fish are ok, but this place is all about the pizza. I had a perfectly thin *boscaiola* pizza with mushrooms, salsiccia, cheese and tomato – but I began, in the Roman style, with a *supplì* (rice ball) and fried zucchini blossoms.

The place has strong connections to Rome's film world. Pictures of Anna Magnani and the director Luchino Visconti hang on the walls. The lunch scene in *Bellissima* was staged here; Magnani leaves her food and lets herself be seduced – to a certain point – among the tall plants beside the river, by the stylish Walter Chiari; he pretends to be a producer, but is in fact only an insignificant worker in the film industry. Anna Magnani plays along so that her young daughter might win a major role in an upcoming film. But the girl is not *bellissima* enough to anyone except her mother. This comedy makes a point about film and vanity.

Ten minutes' walk from the metro Basilica San Paolo.

O *Open every day except Tuesday*
A *Via Ostiense 178; Ostiense*
T *+39 06 574 1172*
W *www.albiondotevere.it*

DA REMO

I haven't made many visits here during my time in Rome, for the simple reason that Remo is a relatively small place that fills up quickly and doesn't take reservations. Instead you have to hang around by the door when they open at 7.30pm. Each return visit is a triumph though, especially if you luck into an outdoor table in the square.

When you enter, the first thing you see is a pizza counter with a wood-fired oven. The pizza a bit smaller than at neighboring **Nuovo Mondo** (p. 106) and might have the occasional blackened edge. But the place, which consists of two rooms, feels genuine with its rickety wooden tables, covered with white paper, and wine served in simple carafes.

Despite its spartan decor, or maybe because of it, there is a distinct feeling of coziness here. The cheap beer and white wine from Rome's Frascati and Marino wine districts are flowing. Regulars talk loudly and gesture wildly, and with tables that only have a few inches between them, it mean that the evening can easily turn into one long Fellini film, in the best way. If you're a Lazio supporter you should keep it to yourself, because this is smack bang in the middle of Testaccio's AS

Roma area, where the football team was first created in 1927. For those who don't feel like eating pizza I recommend the house *melanzane alla Parmigiana*, a gratin of sliced fried eggplant, thick tomato sauce, mozzarella and parmesan. Simple, yet incredibly difficult to do perfectly. Remo's version is one of Rome's best. The most fun thing about this place is the people and the everyday life on display. Remo is a perfect Roman scene, reminding you that the city is one big eternal show.

O *Open every day except Sunday*
A *Piazza di Santa Maria Liberatrice 44; Testaccio*
T *+39 06 574 6270*

ER PANONTO
This place is simple and has a large, popular garden. It serves classic Roman thin-crust pizza. A big plus is the enormous buffet of small dishes and vegetables that many guests choose to have before their pizza. Take a walk first in this pretty and unique part of town from the 1920s. Just 10 minutes' walk from metro Garbatella.

O *Open every evening*
A *Via Enrico Cravero 8/10; Garbatella*
T *+39 06 513 5022*

GRAZIE A DIO È VENERDÌ
Thin Roman pizza that stays soft and smooth. Good value for money – the standard pizza is gigantic. The house special pizza (Thank god it's Friday!) with cheese, zucchini flowers and bolete mushrooms is an excellent choice from the seriously long pizza menu. In the Monti neighborhood near metro Cavour.

O *Open every evening*
A *Via dei Capocci 1; Monti*

IL CAPRICCIO
In between the Pantheon and Piazza Navona, this decent little pizzeria has managed to hold on. Here you get pizza by the slice. Today the industry is crammed with jokers who use a fixed price of 3–4 euros for a little pizza slice. But you should only pay for what you buy when served pizza by the slice – which is to say, pizza slices should be put on a scale and weighed. Here nearly every sort of pizza costs 2 euro per 100 grams (3.5 ounces). The pizza is well made and thin – not like at many other places these days, which intentionally make their pizza crusts thick and bready for tourists, and then charge more. I'm not promising the best pizza in town, but this is better than ok. Try it with thinly sliced potatoes or with *funghi e salsiccia*. Pizza covered in a thick layer of eggplant gratin is also quite good.

I often come here if I'm in a hurry, but the place does have tables where you can sit down. This costs 1 euro extra, but if you're in a large group you don't have to pay it.

O *Open every day 10am–11pm*
A *Via Giustiniani 18C; Center*

Yasser Abouelella comes from Egypt and has for many years made pizza at Grazie a Dio è Venerdì

The menu at Grazie a Dio è Venerdì is enormous

103

XII PIZZA WARS ON THREE FRONTS

When it comes to eating good pizza, many people think the toppings are most important. But the truth is that it all comes down to the dough and therefore the pizza's base: just thick enough, not too bready and not too thin – otherwise the pizza burns too easily.

There's an ongoing pizza war in the capital city. In Rome, there are three main schools of thought when it comes to what makes the best pizza.

The Neapolitan pizza crust is soft and has a high fluffy edge. Unbeatable if it's done right: a little yeast in the dough and a long rising time, if possible 24 hours, but certain cult places boast of even longer rising times. Only if the dough is properly yeasted can the pizza be baked for 90 seconds in an oven where the temperature is well above 400 degrees Fahrenheit (200 degrees Celsius). Otherwise the pizza starts to take on the consistency of a rubber sole. The way of making pizza in Naples has drawn a cult following. In December 2017 UNESCO awarded world heritage status to the art of making Neapolitan pizza to preserve the practice for future generations.

The Roman pizza is exactly the opposite: thin and crispy, but it should still be elastic. It doesn't concern itself with rolling pins. But some people "cheat" by adding a little oil to the dough to make it smoother, despite the fact that this is technically against the rules.

Pizza toppings are always classic. There aren't many places in Rome that serve pizza with bananas. Dessert pizza with Nutella is extremely rare. The classics like *capricciosa* and *quattro stagioni* dominate, as does pizza with *funghi* (mushrooms). Margherita remains eternal: the pizza is named after Italy's first queen and was created in Naples

in 1889. In it, the three familiar colors of the Italian flag mingle: red tomatoes, white mozzarella and green basil leaves.

The world-famous pizza Napoli remains an enigma. Often it's tomato, mozzarella, anchovies and oregano. You can order a pizza Napoli in Naples; there it's often pizza *marinara* with tomato sauce, oregano, anchovies and sometimes black olives. In southern Italy it's sometimes called Roman pizza. Order that in Rome though and the waiter will stand there, confused.

The pizza war remains a matter of taste, where, as a pizza lover, you must choose a favorite between Rome and

Grazie a Dio è Venerdì (p. 102)

Naples. But don't miss the nice variation *pizza a taglio*, pizza by the slice – the third front in the pizza war. Pizza sold by the slice should never have a fixed price because that means it's a tourist trap; slices should always be sold by weight. You point at the counter to the one you want and the pizza vendor weighs it, which works well even if you don't speak a word of Italian. You eat the pizza standing up, or you can fill up a whole pizza box and take it with you out to one of Rome's many parks.

A quick survey of Rome's pizzerias clearly demonstrates this is the hardest of all the culinary arts. Only one in ten pizzas approaches perfection, because the room temperature, wood, sourdough, flour and humidity all affect the result. Pizza that's baked early in the evening can be a totally different thing from one that's baked two hours later. And most important of all are the pizza baker's skills and mood.

Italy remains, of course, a safe bet. There isn't a single Pizza Hut in all the country, and it's very unlikely that one will ever open. No Roman would tolerate such misery. Remember that pizza is a dish that is made at night in Rome, although there are exceptions.

IVO A TRASTEVERE

A large pizzeria with perfect dough. It has properly refreshed itself and has introduced pasta dishes and even main courses to the menu. But there are better places to go for those dishes; here you should eat pizza. The offerings are enormous and logically divided into red- and white-sauce pizzas. I tried something new: pizza King with bolete mushrooms, pork, smoked provalone and lightly smoked speck from Alto Adige in northern Italy. It sounded good, but turned out to be much too rich and fatty.

The ground rule is that the simplest pizzas are often the best – the classics – but you can happily try them with radicchio and gorgonzola or *fiori e alici* with zucchini blossoms and anchovies. There's also a large selection of crostini: the toasted bread slices covered with melted mozzarella, mushrooms and Italian ham are a good alternative to pizza or just for something to share as an appetizer.

The place was totally renovated a few years ago and has become much cozier. In the renovation all the TV screens disappeared. I thought the reason was because there were loud arguments between Roma and Lazio's football supporters, but I heard the truth from a waiter: "Signore, we have finished with TV because people would sit here the whole night and just watch the matches". So, Ivo is no longer a football pizzeria. The icon of a soccer ball, however, remains on the menu outside.

O *Open every day except Tuesday, 5pm–1am*
A *Via di San Francesco a Ripa 158; Trastevere*
T *+39 06 581 7082*

NUOVO MONDO

In this giant pizzeria with seating for 200 people you can always find a table, even on a Saturday night. Nuovo Mondo is a pillar of pizza-making in the formerly working-class neighborhood of Testaccio. The interior is spartan and without atmosphere. But the people are always fun and genuine in this part of town. Here there's a whole team of pizza bakers behind the counter. Their process is coordinated to the tiniest detail. First the baker, with nimble fingers, forms the round thin pizza bases at furious speed. The next baker calls for all the various toppings, while a third takes care of the oven so no pizza gets burned. The crust is

Architecturally famous post office in the Testaccio neighborhood

thin and large, without ever getting dry or the least bit doughy.

I recommend the pizza with bitter arugula which matched perfectly with gorgonzola. We also tasted *crostino con alici*, toasted bread slices that are layered over each other with mozzarella and anchovies. My favorite remains *fiori e alici* – pizza with mozzarella, zucchini blossoms and anchovies. It is just the right amount of salt to go well with the light Italian beer.

- **O** *Open every day except Monday, 6.30pm–12am*
- **A** *Via Amerigo Vespucci 15; Testaccio*
- **T** *+39 06 574 6004*

MARGARÌ
A mix of Roman and Neapolitan traditions. The pizza is just thick enough and perfectly baked. Many people start with the house potato croquettes, fried *supplì* (rice balls) or zucchini flowers filled with mozzarella and anchovies. Here it's possible to sit outside, far beyond the main tourist drag in the Marranella quarter that borders the trendy Pigneto. It's also cheap. The easiest way here is the old train from Roma Laziali (Via Giovanni Giolitti) to the stop Casilina-Alessi. From there it's an easy walk, though a map on your cellphone is recommended.

- **O** *Open every evening*
- **A** *Via Marco Vincenzo Coronelli 30; Marranella – alongside Via Casilina*
- **T** *+39 06 217 00650*
- **W** *www.margari.it*

PIZZERIA BRUTO
Pizzeria Bruto is modern even though it has existed for a long time, but it's never been "trendy". Regulars here eat in the semi-fashionable Trieste neighborhood, but that's not what draws me here. I come here because the place makes, in my opinion, Rome's best Roman pizza: thin, but never dry; tasty, elastic dough and good toppings. Beyond classic pizzas (like the super good Napoli I had last time with tomato, olives, anchovies and capers) there are creative pizzas like *bedda matri* (pretty mamma) with buffalo mozzarella, *caponata* and basil. While "flower power" is a Margherita with buffalo mozzarella, zucchini blossoms, capers, anchovies, arugula and *'nduja* (soft, spreadable, strongly flavored salami from Calabria).

Among the appetizers, I recommend *polpette di melanzane* (fried eggplant balls).

There's a large outdoor seating area open in summer. Bus 38 from Roma Termini to the stop at Trieste/Trasimeno.

- **O** *Open every evening except Monday*
- **A** *Via Malta 12–14; Trieste – adjacent to Piazza Caprera*
- **T** *+39 06 855 7440*
- **W** *www.bruto.roma.it*

PIZZERIA ITALIA

Undeniably Rome's best pizza by the slice at the right price. **Gabriele Bonci** (p. 109) is indeed an artist, and although this is the standard street-pizzeria, the pizza itself isn't standard. It is exceptionally good! The dough is thin and light, crisp without being dry. And being light, it's also cheaper (because you pay by weight). Here most of the pizza slices cost around 1.50 euro per 100 grams (3.5 ounces). But pizza with shrimp or smoked salmon is of course more expensive, as is the one with bolete mushrooms. The simple classic pizzas are almost always the best, like pizza with mushrooms and tomatoes or gorgonzola and radicchio. A new option for me was pizza with smoked provolone and gold pumpkin.

Here there are also stuffed pizzas made with focaccia. The fillings are plentiful, like prosciutto and mozzarella or lightly salted air-dried bresaola with *rughetta* (arugula). And yes, the focaccia bread is even filled with sweet ricotta, Nutella and garnished with confectioners' sugar. As a pizza traditionalist I tasted this dessert pizza a little reluctantly. It turned out to be a proper culinary knockout; sinfully good. Next time I have a party don't bring any cakes, because Nutella pizza with the light sting of salt from the bread is the most delicious thing I've eaten, and cakes will no longer do.

The shop is small, so avoid the lunch rush. It has been 30 years since Palmerino Amicone founded this little place, and his kids continue to it run today. Honor Rome's premier pizza baker with a visit. It is definitely worth the effort to get here.

- **O** *Open every day except Sunday, 9am–9pm*
- **A** *Corso d'Italia 103; Salario – near Porta Pia*
- **T** *+39 06 442 49771*

PIZZERIA PANATTONI – AI MARMI

The simplest way for Romans to socialize is to go out for a beer and a pizza. It should also be inexpensive. Panattoni, which lies along Trastevere's main road, has been around since the 1930s and has not changed much. The pizza is wafer-thin and maybe isn't the city's best, but the experience is super Roman. In summer the seating area expands to cover the whole sidewalk, but if there are still no free tables then you have to sit indoors. It is cozy and fun if you can entertain yourself with people-watching. In this large room there are youngsters, big extended families, and the newly in-love couple out to enjoy a beer and a *capricciosa*.

The Panattoni family has run the place for a long time and has introduced occasional new items, like pizza with bananas and pizza with bresaola and arugula. If you ask anyone in Rome about Pizzeria Panattoni nobody knows where it is, but if you say *L'obitorio* (mortuary) everyone knows it. That nickname has hung around as long as the harsh fluorescent tube lighting on the ceiling and the white marble tables that are still here. This is why the place is also called

Ai marmi (marble). In summertime you can eat pizza here until at least 1.30am.

- **O** *Open every evening except Wednesday*
- **A** *Viale del Trastevere 53; Trastevere*
- **T** *+39 06 580 0919*

PIZZARIUM BONCI

Over the past decade Gabriele Bonci has become Rome's major pizza guru. Bonci knows all about stone-ground flour and sourdough that has existed for generations. "Pizza is one of the noblest of all the kitchen arts. Here all the chefs' experiences meet all the bakers'", as his slogan goes. This is pizza at the highest level: pizza with tomato, mozzarella and anchovies from Cantabrico; or pizza with whole-fried Tuscan piglet, *cinta senese*; or a variation with oven-baked potatoes, black truffle and *lardo di Colonnata* – bacon

that's spiced with pepper and rosemary and then stored in porous gray marble sinks in the little village of Colonnata in northern Tuscany. These are just a few of Bonci's fantastic dishes which he serves with a piece of perfectly baked bread, also made in an electric oven.

In step with its culinary success, the place has become elegant and modern, decorated with glass and light-colored wood. The counters that display the pizza on offer by the slice are an artwork in themselves – a perfect still-life in Gaudi colors. The place is still minimal. The queue winds all the way around the pizzeria and there is only one pair of benches to sit on outside. In the Prati area just adjacent to metro Cipro.

P.S. Not far from here, on Via del Trionfale 36, lies Bonci's bread shop which is also worth a visit.

- **O** *Open every day 11am–10pm, except Sunday between 4pm–6pm; avoid the lunch rush*
- **A** *Via della Meloria 43; Prati*
- **T** *+39 06 397 45416*

PIZZA FORUM

The best Neapolitan pizza in town is just a block away from the Colosseum. Romans have rightly been resistant to the Neapolitan take on pizza, with its tall and fluffy crust. They feel it's too heavy to be eaten and digested late in the evening. But here you are in safe hands. The bakers here are all from Naples. You'll find all the classics, but remember that just as there are danish pastries in Denmark, so there is pizza Napoli in Naples. That pizza is called Napoli for the sake of the Romans – to appease the city's residents.

Take a Margherita with red tomatoes, white mozzarella and green basil: the colors of the Italian flag. According to legend, this pizza was created in Naples in 1889 and named after Italy's then queen, Margherita of Savoy.

As a starter you should share a portion of *angioletti* (tiny angels) which consists of fried strips of pizza dough with tomato sauce and a little shaved cheese. The food is at the center of this restaurant and there's even a selection of Neapolitan pasta dishes. The kitschy decor is however a little sad; it's better to choose one of the many outdoor tables if the weather allows.

O *Open every day for lunch and dinner*
A *Via di San Giovanni in Laterano 34–36; Center, adjacent to Colosseum*
T *+39 06 775 91158*
W *www.pizzaforumroma.com*

―――――

PORTO FLUVIALE PIZZERIA

This place is named after the city's ancient harbor, where all goods were unloaded 2000 years ago. Today, the restaurant sits in a modern neighborhood, and Porto Fluviale is a multi-zoned food city, with a bar, trattoria and pizzeria. The last is the best, offering a modern take on pizza. The crust has a flavor, elasticity and consistency that you find at few other places in town. The secret is the organic stone-ground flour and 72-hour rising time. My pizza Napoli with cheese, tomato and anchovies was perfect and I got capers as an add-on topping.

The list of pizzas is just big and imaginative enough to keep you satisfied. Here you can choose whether you want pizza that is Roman-thin or Neapolitan-style – thicker with tall and fluffy edges – which costs extra. We started with *arancine*

(fried rice balls): one with chili, pumpkin and dill, and one with leek, spinach and fontina cheese. A plus for the desserts: crispy crumble pie with soft apples and cinnamon. Seven minutes' walk from the metro Piramide.

O *Open every day 12.30–3.30pm and 7.30pm–1.30am*
A *Via del Porto Fluviale 22; between Via Ostiense and the Tiber*
T *+39 06 574 3199*
W *www.portofluviale.com*

―――――

PUMMARELLA

A little pizza shop with a large selection, in the Prati neighborhood, adjacent to the metro Ottaviano. The place was recently opened by two enthusiasts, Costantino and Davide, both with roots in southern Italy. They do exceedingly well-made pizza at a craftsman's level, with a very long rising time. Many of the ingredients come from Apulia, like the creamy burrata, olive oil and tomatoes.

This is also a great place for pizzas by the slice, to try different bases and toppings. We tried a Sicilian variation called *focaccia Messinese* with tomatoes, anchovies and the local, fresh sheep's cheese *tuma*. There's also stuffed pizzas with onion, anchovies and small raisins.

Sometimes they serve a single pasta dish, like Apulia's ear-shaped pasta *orecchiette* with *cime di rapa* (fresh broccoli rabe). We also had a butterfly-light *panzerotto* (little fried pizza) which was most like a dumpling, filled with tomatoes and mozzarella – the two ingredients that together form the eatery's Italian name.

This is a place for enthusiasts who want to discover a whole new pizza scene. There are only a few tables.

O *Open every day 11am–10.30pm*
A *Via Andrea Doria 10; Prati*
T *+39 33 327 84848*
W *www.facebook.com/pummarellaroma/*

SFORNO

Yep, this place even does typical pizza, but everything is special here. The dough is perfect and feels butterfly-light both on the tongue and in the belly, partly because it's sourdough.

Stefano Callegari likes to experiment. The pizza Greenwich comes from the English tradition of eating Stilton with port wine, or, on festive occasions, of marinating the cheese in port wine like a sort of potted cheese. This pizza is one of Sforno's prettiest, with mozzarella and crumbled Stilton and garnished after baking with a reduction of select ruby port. Here they use real buffalo mozzarella, which is hard to set directly on a pizza because the cheese contains so much moisture that it can turn the pizza into a white sea. Sforno has solved the problem by shaving the mozzarella into strips a day before and letting them drain properly.

The pizza that made the place famous is called *cacio e pepe* (cheese and black pepper). It is also the name of one of Rome's simplest and most beloved pasta dishes. In order for the recipe to work as a pizza, the pizza has to be properly moist when it comes out of the oven. Callegari achieves this by baking the pizza with an extra-high edge and placing ice on it before it goes in the oven. After 90 seconds (a longer baking time than Sforno's usual pizzas) the pizza is fully baked but still damp from the melted ice. The pizza is then served with a generous layer of shaved *pecorino Romano* mixed with a lot of black pepper. Drizzled olive oil completes the pizza.

Start with one of the house *supplì* (Roman rice balls). They come in flavors like *amatriciana* sauce with pork, broccoli and pecorino or gorgonzola with radicchio. There is a large outdoor seating area here. Metro A to Subaugusta makes it easy to find this place.

P.S. Callegari together with his colleague Antonio Prattico has opened **Tonda** (p. 111), a new sister-pizzeria in northern Rome with the same menu. Here you can find the much talked about *trapizzini*: filled pizza bread that resembles the triangular bar sandwiches *tramezzini*. Try it filled with ragu on *trippa* (tripe), tongue with green sauce or *parmigiana light* (eggplant casserole). A large top-notch selection of different types of beer; the Italian Ducato from Emilia gets well deserved cult status – it's a beer that's made in Giuseppe Verdi's home village of Roncole.

O *Open every evening from 7.45pm*
A *Via Statilio Ottato 110–116; Tuscolana*
T *+39 06 715 46118*
W *www.sforno.it*

TONDA

Get here on bus 90 from Roma Termini to the bus stop Nomentana/Val D'Ossola. Make sure you book a table! Tonda lies a bit far away so you don't want to arrive and hear that there's no room.

O *Open every evening from 7.45pm*
A *Via Valle Corteno 31; Montesacro*
T *+39 06 81 80 960*

XIII

GO AND SWIM

Benito Mussolini came from Predappio, relatively close to the Adriatic Sea. He was a diligent swimmer, and made swimming part of fascism's propaganda when he became Italy's dictator in 1925. Romans have him to thank for their easy access to the ocean. In 1924 Mussolini championed the railway that connected Rome with Ostia, promoting the belief that the city would once again stretch all the way to the sea, and that ancient Rome's harbor town Ostia could again become part of the Eternal City.

Today the train line is a part of the underground metro. You have to change at Piramide. The end station in Ostia – Cristoforo Colombo – is right by the sea. And those eager to settle down with their beach umbrellas and sun chairs have *stabilimento* Venezia at their feet. *Stabilimento* means public beach – it's a section of beach that's run by a family or private owner but with public-use rights.

9pm and the last train back to Rome leaves right after 11pm, so make sure you don't get stranded on the beach!

Part of the beach is a nudist beach. Oasi Naturista is the only one authorized in all of Lazio. It is, however, not compulsory to sunbathe and swim naked. Each *stabilimento* has its own clientele who vary radically within some few hundred meters of beach: young families with kids, teens, couples, bodybuilders, Brazilians – a Rio in miniature, if you will.

The best and most relaxed of the *stabilimento* are Mediterraneo and Dar Zagaja – in the Roman dialect, "one who falters". The legendary Gaspare Vichi, known as Zagaja, was a big local personality who ran an eatery on the beach. Sadly he died in 2010, and today his children run the place. For the last few years Dar Zagaja has been the safest bet for a place to eat directly on the beach. You can step right in wearing your swimsuit, at least for lunch. It's perfect for an *aperitivo* while the sun sets into the sea before you. I have eaten here loads of times. They serve good mussels, risotto with scampi, grilled fish and a large *frittura* with shrimp and octopus. The house wine is accompanied by a modest selection of decent white wines. Open daily during high season (May–September) and sometimes on weekends the rest of the year if the weather is good. To book a table, call +39 06 563 05026.

Romans swim here, but the water is far from crystal-clear. For a nicer swimming spot I recommend taking the train south to Formia and then the bus to Gaeta and the beach Serapo. Pretty and picturesque, the little village Sperlonga is all white houses and a long sandy beach.

Venezia (tel. +39 06 564 70166) even has its own good restaurant and a large pool.

The beach, stretching to the city Torvaianica, is about 10 miles (15 kilometers) long. After around 6 miles (10 kilometers) you get to the free beach called Il buco (the hole). This beach is very popular in summer when Romans come in the tens of thousands. It is often impossible to park a car, so trains and buses are best. In summer, May–September, take beach-bus line 07. The last buses leave the beach at

XIV FOOD AND ROMAN FILM

The first thing I think of when it comes to Italian film and food is of course Marco Ferreri's *La Grande Bouffe*, where four men eat themselves to death. Few directors can provoke like Ferreri. But that film was set in Paris.

In Vittorio De Sica's neo-realistic masterpiece *Ladri di biciclette* (*The Bicycle Thief*), the father, Antonio (Lamberto Maggiorani), takes his young son Bruno (Enzo Staiola who became world-famous for the role) to a fine restaurant by the river. Because he doesn't have money, he orders a carafe of white wine and the simplest of dishes: mozzarella in carrozza – two slices of bread dipped in egg with milk and flour, then fried with mozzarella in the middle; poor-man's food to use up old bread.

Ettore Scola is undoubtedly the director who devoted himself most to food in his films. It plays an important role in a lot of his movies. Conversations play out often around the dinner table, like in *The Family* or in *La Terrazza,* where lost leftist-intellectuals talk over each other rather than to each other while a giant buffet is served on the large terrace.

In Scola's earlier film *A Drama of Jealousy* Marcello Mastroianni and Giancarlo Giannini compete for Monica Vitti's favor. It gets dramatic and many of the film's scenes play out in a pizzeria where Giannini works. But first and foremost is *We All Loved Each Other So Much* where the food plays a starring role; or more accurately, the trattoria. Scola depicts a post-war Rome where Stefania Sandrelli and her three suitors sit at a neighborhood restaurant and only hear each other, despite the intense outside city noise. They are deep inside an isolated cinematic romance bubble.

It became clear that Scola had a lot more to say about the traditional trattoria 25 years later when he made *La Cena*. Here Fanny Ardant is the elegant restaurant owner who takes care of her regulars. The film was rooted in reality – each Wednesday the restaurant **Otello** reserved its one large dining room for Scola and his film friends. Directors, scriptwriters, actors, critics and journalists would meet there.

That tradition is gone. Scola and fellow director and Otello regular Mario Monicelli are dead, as are many of their collaborators and scriptwriters. Otello is still around, but is a shadow of its former self.

Also gone is the city's beloved Alberto Sordi, a folk hero for his countless comedies. The scene in *An American in Rome* where he eats a giant plate of spaghetti is probably the best advertisement ever made for Italian pasta. Sordi's character Ferdinando Mericoni is, of course, super Roman and a man who dreams of the USA and becoming American – after WWII Italy was among the most pro-American countries in all of Europe.

Federico Fellini has also been good for cinematic pasta binges. In his love letter to the Italian capital, simply and aptly titled *Roma*, he shows how a young Fellini arrived in Rome. He arrives in the middle of the Trastevere neighborhood's big Festa de' Noantri and is shocked over the Romans' eating habits – dining on intestines drenched in dark-red tomato sauce.

The American author Gore Vidal makes an appearance in another of the film's scenes. He lived for a while in Rome. In the film Vidal says, "Rome is the city of illusions. It is not a coincidence that the Church, government and cinema are here. They each create illusions, just like you and I. We're getting closer and closer to the end of the world, because of too many people, too many cars, poisons. And what better city than Rome, which has been reborn so often; what place could be more peaceful to wait for the end of the world? It's the ideal city for waiting to see if it will really come to an end or not."

So said Vidal. The year was 1972 and I had already been to Rome. The Eternal City continues to live, if not as carefree as it once was.

XV AMONG VOLCANOES AND WINE

The Castelli Romani area, where much of Lazio's wine is produced, is one of Rome's most popular excursions, because it's less than 20 miles (30 kilometers) from the city. Many of the small villages have now grown into small cities. Don't come here on a weekend in spring because you'll get stuck in an unending queue of cars on the small curvy roads. Same applies in fall, when large wine festivals are held.

In the kitchen at Taverna dello Spunito (p. 123)

The area is volcanic, but the last volcanic activity took place 5000 years ago. The beautiful, deep Lake Albano is a volcano crater lake. There's a swimming beach on one shore, but the lake is dangerous, with strong currents.

High above the lake is Castel Gandolfo, where the pope has his summer residence – although he rarely uses it. The residence, which also comprises the beautiful Barberini Gardens is open for visitors. Tickets can be bought on site, but I recommend buying tickets through the Vatican's website, under the section "Villas and gardens". Villa Barberini, which contains gardens and archaeological remains, offers a ticket that costs 20 euro, with a family discount. You must join a tour, which take place in a small eco-friendly car. The pope's apostolic palace at the central square is open from 8.30am–1pm, closed most Sundays. On Saturday it's open until 4.30pm and entry costs 10 euro.

There are many other places to see and visit. Lilla Ariccia has a magnificent duke's palace that belongs to the rich Tuscan noble family Chigi, from which Pope Alessandro VII of the 1600s came. The square and church across from the palace were designed by the Baroque architect Gian Lorenzo Bernini. Ariccia is known for its *porchetta* (roasted pig), spiced with rosemary. It's sold by weight in slices everywhere. Ariccia also has many *frasche* (wine cottages), which are marked by a bough outside. Where there are wine cottages, there the owner serves his own wine, but anything you want to eat, you need to bring along yourself.

The small, picturesque town Nemi is also bordered by a volcanic lake. The town is known for its *fragoline di bosco* (strawberries), which are raised in greenhouses and available year-round. I never eat strawberries in Italy, they have no flavor. But Nemi's strawberries taste just like the ones I ate in my childhood. Buy and enjoy. Or try the strawberry pastry at the bar. Vanilla ice-cream or whipped cream with strawberries are delicious. The Italians usually eat them with pressed lemon and sugar.

It is hard to eat well in Castelli Romani. The restaurants are large and often cater for parties and weddings. In Genzano though I recommend the no-reservations **Pelliccione** at Piazza Giuseppe Mazzini in the middle of town (tel. +39 06 936 4480), with large portions and lots to choose from. Avoid Sundays if possible. The town is known for its light farmhouse bread; a good portion of it is sold in Rome.

At the slightly anonymous but inexpensive town of Grottaferrata I have always eaten very well. **Taverna dello Spuntino** (p. 123) is a delight when it comes to food and atmosphere. Simpler and more charming is **La Briciola di Adriana** on Via Gabriele D'Annuzio 12 (tel. +39 06 945 9338).

On a glowing warm July evening when the temperature nears 100 degrees Fahrenheit (40 degrees Celsius) it can be nice to escape from Rome. On such nights when I want a very simple, authentic and cool place we usually get a group together

and go to **La Selvotta** (Via Selvotta 43, tel. +39 06 932 4521) which lies in the midst of a chestnut forest above Ariccia. It's a very simple restaurant, but it can get a little awkward if it's busy. You can buy cold cuts, sausage, roasted pig, olives and bread directly from the storehouse; warm dishes like bruschetta and bucatini *all'amatriciana* you order at the table; same if you want a grilled steak and a tomato salad.

You can't reserve a table, and the place is not easy to find – you need a functioning GPS. Open from April to October for lunch and dinner. The weather must be good though, because you eat outside.

To see Castelli Romani properly you need a car, but to get to the towns like Frascati, Castel Gandolfo and Marino Laziale (as the station is called) you can take a train from Roma Termini.

JUST OUTSIDE OF TOWN

LA SCORPACCIATA

At the quay next to the sea, the fishing boats gather. This is where you'll find Rome's freshest fish, although if you want to get technical, Fiumicino these days is actually its own independent municipality. It's five minutes' drive from the airport, so if you have a late afternoon flight it's the perfect spot for lunch before you drop off your rental car.

In Fiumicino there are many elegant bistros. La Scorpacciata, which means "blowout", is a simple little trattoria.

The pasta dishes are, as is often the case, much better than the main dishes, even though the plate of fried shrimp and octopus was perfect. For 22 euro you get six seafood appetizers that change daily and one pasta dish. The best is rigatoni in tomato sauce with mussels and a generous amount of grated pecorino. The egg pasta *tonnarelli* comes with mussels, clams and fresh tomatoes. The wider pasta fettuccine is served with shrimp and tomatoes. Portions are meant for *camionisti*, as they say in Italian – truck drivers – so it can be wise to order just a few starters and a pasta. Seldom have I eaten better and cheaper by the sea, and the easy-going Massimiliano who runs the trattoria makes you feel like you're a regular from the first visit. There are only a few outdoor tables and a very limited wine list. Book early for the weekends because the place is small.

🄾 *Open every day except Monday*
🄰 *Via Orbetello 10; Fiumicino*
🅃 *+39 06 650 48266*

L'ORTO DI ALBERICO

Along Via Appia Antica the city comes to a sudden stop. Bounded by the Roman aqueduct, a swathe of countryside opens up unexpectedly. This is not *agriturismo* (agricultural tourism) and not an ordinary restaurant, but a farmyard in the country that welcomes dining guests. The owners are not just anyone; the new generation that runs the place comes from the family Antinori – wine producers in Tuscany since 1385 – and in current times from the noble family Boncompagni Ludovisi. The grandfather Alberico thrives when on his tractor and takes care of the mill.

Nearly everything here is produced on the farm: bread, fruit and vegetables, pasta, olive oil, fresh ricotta and both red and white wine. To settle down at an outdoor table on a summer evening and see the sun disappear behind the cone-covered pine trees in this ancient landscape is a pleasure. The food is made with that day's produce. A dish of crispy

Alessia Antinori at L'Orto di Alberico

fried sage from the spice garden lands on the table. Exciting pasta dishes follow, like *gricia* (crispy pork) with chestnut cream or cocoa pasta that's shaped into ravioli and filled with ricotta and asparagus. *Cramble salato* is a salt-crumble pie with parmesan and rosemary in the dough. Over the pie are strewn a selection of vegetables like peppers, eggplants and diced carrot. But there's also meat on the menu, like lean and well-roasted duck breast. The kitchen uses an extremely delicate hand with spices and salt. Only 1 mile (1.5 kilometers) from the airport in Ciampino. Opening times vary depending on the season.

O *Open Friday for aperitivo, Saturday dinner and Sunday lunch*
A *Via di Fioranello 34; near Appia Antica and Ciampino airport*
T *+39 34 080 88211*
W *www.ortodialberico.it*
E *info@ortodialberico.it*

L'OSTERIA DELL'OROLOGIO
An elegant seafood restaurant at the harbor in Fiumicino, but highly personal and accommodating; you feel at home after just one visit here. Homemade bread arrives warm at the

table accompanied by a delicious organic olive oil. Americo Quattrociocchi's oil from Alatri in Lazio tastes feather-light, but is at the same time balanced with a slightly bitter aftertaste.

The kitchen is small so if you order a tasting menu with antipasti expect to wait a bit. The *panzanella* (a Tuscan bread salad) looks like toast with chopped beets, but the flavor reveals that it's actually chopped tuna with red onion that's been garnished with golden peppers. Spaghetti with sea urchins and strips of creamy buffalo mozzarella is a flavor sensation. The pastas arrive with a glass cover and have been smoked while cooking, which elevates the dishes to another level.

The chef is Marco Claroni and he has run the place for eight years with his wife Gerarda Fini who is the sommelier. It isn't much help to recommend individual dishes, because they change often. I hope that you'll find the honey-tossed fresh figs with *sapa* (cooked-down wine juice) on the menu, served with fig ice-cream flavored with cocoa and the fresh cheese robiola. When served it's finished with a generous spritz of grappa that the waiter has in an aluminum spray bottle. Good value for a place at this level. Tasting menu with nine dishes costs 60 euro. You need a car to reach the restaurant comfortably, otherwise it's 10 minutes in a taxi from the airport in Fiumicino.

O *Open every day except Monday; in summer open every day except lunch Tuesday to Thursday*
A *Via della Torre Clementina 114; Fiumicino*
T *+39 06 650 5251 or +39 34 751 79051*
W *www.osteriadellorologio.net*

TAVERNA DELLO SPUNTINO

Castelli Romani, Rome's wine castles, is among the city's most popular excursions. Villages like Marino, Frascati, Albano and Ariccia are treasured by many Romans. Grottaferrata is the smallest village; it's slightly more affluent with some really good restaurants. At the top of the list is this rustic but refined eatery whose name literally means "mouth bits", culinary irony at its highest level.

The portions are beautifully plated and made in a kitchen that wouldn't even know how to pronounce *nouvelle cuisine*. The house pork with melon or buffalo mozzarella is a traditional start. A salad of bolete mushrooms and parmesan is a more adventurous way to start, if it's in season. The meat dishes are the feature of the restaurant, but do try the house tortellini which is egg pasta filled with vegetables. Vegetarians have an enormous selection of dishes to choose from and can put together a giant plate by combining them. We had trouble choosing between roasted suckling pig and deboned oven-roasted rabbit served sliced and stuffed with juniper berries and small olives from Liguria. *Guancia* (beef cheeks) cooked in red wine makes the choice even more difficult, as did the grilled lamb cutlets. I finally settled on turkey stuffed with an omelet and asparagus, while my friend tried guinea fowl with wild fennel.

We drank a full-bodied locally-produced red wine, Vigna del Vassallo, from Colle Picchioni in the neighboring town of Marino. We had no room for dessert, but we couldn't turn down the house's vanilla ice-cream with *fragoline di*

Fresh ricotta with red pepper

bosco, cultivated strawberries raised in a greenhouse in the village of Nemi, which have become justly famous.

The eatery is a triumph for Basilio Fortini and his wife Anna. It is rustic and simultaneously elegant. Beyond the perfect food, they've also brought enormous style to the interior decor. From the ceiling hang sausages, hams and glittering red tomato vines. The table for four people can be shared among guests – in the middle there are such high fruit baskets and flower arrangements that we could neither see nor hear our tablemates.

Don't miss the gigantic wine cellar, deep beneath the dining room. The cellar has several floors that have been carved out of the mountain – something most buildings have in this wine district because

it rests upon an old volcanic stone that was easy to chisel out.

Those who eat dinner and don't want to drive back to Rome, or who want to spend a weekend here, can book the restaurant's adjacent *locanda*, as such simple *pensiones* used to be called. Today it's a charming family hotel with double rooms (www. locandadellospuntino.com).

Ⓐ *Via Cicerone 22; Grottaferrata*
Ⓣ *+39 06 943 15985 or +39 06 945 9366*
Ⓦ *www.tavernadellospuntino.com*

___

WINE & BARS

"Wine is the song of the earth to the sky"

Luigi Veronelli (1926–2004), wine and food writer

AI TRE SCALINI

This is a wine bar with ancient lineage in trendy Monti along the main street Via Panisperna. There are tables for those who come early or book ahead.

The place is exciting and it is at least as fun to sit at the bar as it is at a table. There's a good selection of wine by the glass, and a little mug with *taralli* (small savoury biscuits) is included in the price. There are also salads, cold cuts with mozzarella and pasta dishes – the last with all certainty warmed up in the microwave. Remember that you are at a wine bar and not a restaurant.

It's predominately locals here. Buy the bar's t-shirt. On the back it says "*Morire si ma non di sete*" (We will die but never of thirst), a good present to take home.

- **O** *Open every day 12.30pm–1am*
- **A** *Via Panisperna 251; Monti*
- **T** *+39 06 48 90 74 95*

ALEMBIC

In the midst of Trastevere's alleys is this drinking lounge, where the timeworn chairs, tables and countertop reflect a galaxy of chandeliers, creating a fantastic lighting effect. The space is a mix of vintage and urban. In the late afternoon sometimes there's live music.

This is first and foremost an evening destination, so it functions as a relatively quiet disco bar that alternates new and old music. It's not for those who are only looking for the latest trends, more for those who want a nice charming place to talk loudly – not frequently on offer in Rome.

It's packed in the evenings. The crowd is young, most are under 30. As nearly always happens in Italy, there's minimal door security and you don't have to have a drink; you can just slip in and hang out if that seems like fun. It's more of a draw in the winter.

Early in the evening you can also eat here, which is quite an adventurous culinary undertaking.

- **O** *Open every day 10.30am–1.30am, Friday to Saturday until 2am*
- **A** *Piazza in Piscinula 51; Trastevere*
- **T** *+39 06 580 0681*
- **W** *www.alembic.it*

BAR DE' PENITENZIERI

Nowhere can you eat worse and more expensively than adjacent to the Vatican and St Peter's Basilica. The reason is crystal clear: swarms of pilgrims and tourists that are tired after a visit to the basilica and museums are ready to throw themselves down at the first place they see along the parade Via della Conciliazione. Don't do it! Go instead to the second cross-street to the left in front of the basilica, Via dei Cavalieri del San Sepolcro. The street immediately changes its name to Via dei Penitenzieri. At number 16 is a perfect little bar with fresh sandwiches – from the three-corner *tramezzini* to proper panini. There's also pizza dough stuffed with anchovies, mozzarella and yellow zucchini blossoms. All at affordable prices. At lunch there's also salad and a daily pasta special to eat at the few tables.

Alessandro and Paola have run the place since 2000 and have renovated everything. There's a full menu for those who want lunch or dinner, but it's totally ok to just have a sandwich and a cappuccino and rest your museum-weary feet. The place describes itself as a wine bar and the wine list is large and well

curated. One of Rome's most important address to inscribe in your memory!

- Ⓞ *Open every day 6am–10pm*
- Ⓐ *Via dei Penitenzieri 16; near the Vatican*
- Ⓣ *+39 06 687 5350*
- Ⓦ *www.winebardepenitenzieri.it*

Pizza dough filled with mozzarella, anchovies and zucchini blossoms at Bar de' Penitenzien (p. 128)

BAR MARANI

In the student area of San Lorenzo this little historic bar stands like an oasis. No music plays and there's no wifi. The balcony with many tables is enveloped in lush greenery. People read the newspaper, students study for exams and a few sit and write. Here time stands still. A coffee, a refreshing lemonade, a martini or a Campari, if you will.

- Ⓞ *Open every day 6am–10pm,*
  except Monday
- Ⓐ *Via dei Volsci 57; San Lorenzo*
- Ⓣ *+39 06 490 019*

CAFFÈ PERÙ

This bar has a special position in the city center – it is the Romans' place. A group of eight friends joined forces to see to it that it gained that reputation. The place is not trendy or especially well-decorated. In fact it's very simple and has been around since the 1930s. But in the evenings, interesting people from the fashion and design worlds come here to hang out and take it easy.

There's a good atmosphere and zero attitude. Plus good wine, including the brilliant Italian bubbly franciacorta. Drinks with a buffet in the evening cost 8 euro.

It's not all that easy to make dinner reservations, but give it a try by telephone or email.

- Ⓞ *Open every day 7am–2am*
- Ⓐ *Via di Monserrato 46; Center*
- Ⓣ *+39 06 687 9548*
- Ⓔ *sasalmeri@yahoo.it*

CAFFÈ PROPAGANDA

This isn't a cafe in the Italian sense – it's more like a French bistro with its decadent, specially decorated setting, where the white rectangular ceramic plates take inspiration from the Paris metro. It's a new concept for Rome. The coffee is, of course, 100 percent Italian and can be sweetened with the hazelnut creme *nocciolino*, if you want. The house "caffè propaganda" includes a macaroon and a couple of Italian cookies. There are also other drinks and food available. An un-Italian place where you can sit for a while with your espresso.

- Ⓞ *Open every day 12pm–2am,*
  except Monday
- Ⓐ *Via Claudia 15; Celio – near*
  the Colosseum
- Ⓦ *www.caffepropaganda.it*

XVI

FOLLOW PASOLINI INTO THE ROMAN NIGHT

Pier Paolo Pasolini (1922–1975) was a prominent figure during the intensely political 1960s and part of the explosive '70s. Today he's primarily remembered as a film director, but Pasolini was also a poet, author, playwright, debater, actor, painter and a guy who loved to play football.

He was a man of contrasts: openly homosexual, communist and Catholic – something that many Italians of the time had a hard time understanding. He created a strong division in the people of his homeland and home city of Rome: there were as many who admired him as who hated him. When the farmer's son Angelo Roncalli (who became Pope John XXIII) died in 1963, Pasolini dedicated his film *Gospel of St Matthew* to the deceased pope.

Because Pasolini was gay and single, he dined out often. He made his debut film *Accattone* (*The Decameron*) in 1961 in the humble, poor outer area called Pigneto – today one of Rome's most trendy areas. The neighborhood is sometimes known as "the new Trastevere", which in my opinion is a slight exaggeration.

The tavern that provided service during filming is no longer here. But Pasolini ate often at **Necci** (p. 140), which had already existed for over three decades even then. In the film there's not a glimpse of the place. It's said that Pasolini thought Necci was an altogether too fussy place to appear in the film, but he filmed a lot along the same street, Via Fanfulla da Lodi.

Among the last things Pasolini did in his life was to visit Stockholm for four days. On Tuesday, 28 October, 1975, he was a guest of the Italian Cultural Institute in Stockholm to speak about his film *Salò*, or *The 120 Days of Sodom*. My colleague Jan E Carlsson from the newspaper *Dagens Nyheter* took his photo.

On November 1, Pasolini returned to Rome and went to **Pommidoro** (p. 87), one of his regular haunts in the student quarter San Lorenzo which he especially liked. He and his best friend Ninetto Davoli met to eat dinner, and along with them were Ninetto's wife and the couple's two sons. Pasolini asked for the bill and paid with a check. He broke up the party just after 10pm because of *faccio tardi* – it was getting late.

The square Piazza della Repubblica near the train station Roma Termini was then a meeting place for male prostitutes. Here Pasolini picked up 17-year-old Giuseppe Pelosi, whom everyone called Pino. They went towards the sea, but because Pelosi hadn't eaten they stopped at the pizzeria **Biondo Tevere** (p. 100).

On the morning of November 2 Pasolini's body was found in a deserted area in Ostia by the sea. The body was badly beaten and had also been run over by Pasolini's own car. Countless investigations and trials resulted from the murder. The general belief is that the slight Pelosi couldn't have acted alone, not least because Pasolini was physically fit, lithe and very strong. But Pino Pelosi was the only one sentenced for the murder.

Pasolini was deeply provocative and had many enemies. If the murder was a hit job, those responsible sleep peacefully today. Pelosi, who had been arrested by police many times on narcotics charges, died in July 2017.

CHIOSTRO DEL BRAMANTE

Bramante's cloister was built in the 1500s and is one of the High Renaissance's most important and prettiest buildings. It is directly adjacent to the church Santa Maria della Pace, a couple of blocks from Piazza Navona. Today the cloister is used regularly for smaller art exhibitions, but you don't have to pay admission to reach the cafeteria. You just step in and go past the queue and then follow a separate staircase up to the next floor. It's a perfect place to sit and read about Rome's history. Enjoy the cloister's courtyard and silence, for there tend to be few visitors. The bar has sandwiches, espresso, cakes and wine. A secluded oasis in the middle of the city center.

O *Open Monday to Friday 10am–7pm, Saturday to Sunday 10am–8pm*
A *Via Arco della Pace 5; Center – near Piazza Navona*
T *+39 06 688 09035*
W *www.chiostrodelbramante.it*

CUL DE SAC

One of Rome's first wine bars that was birthed in the 1970s in line with a new concept known as the *enoteca*. The wine list here has a Biblical format and includes, according to the owner Guy Tamba, more or less 1500 different wines, from simple bottles to large complex red wines and many dessert wines.

When I first started going here they served at most cold cuts with charcuterie and cheese. Today there's a more comprehensive offering with pâtés and warm dishes. On the menu is a perfect pasta *all'amatriciana* and ravioli with ragu of hare, as well as Roman beef roulade and Greek dolmades. And in winter of course hearty warm vegetable soups.

- **O** *Open every day 12pm–12.30am*
- **A** *Piazza di Pasquino 73; Center – near Piazza Navona*
- **T** *+39 06 688 01094*
- **W** *www.enotecaculdesacroma.it*

Guy Tamba at Cul de Sac

DAGNINO

Dagnino can be a lot to handle all at once. But first and foremost it's a place for those who love Sicily. The counter sags with Sicilian cakes and pastries, from the sweet *frutta martorana* (marzipan fruit) to cannoli filled with ricotta and powdered sugar or chocolate and pistachio. There are temptations like shortbread filled with red watermelon jelly and cakes where chocolate and pistachio are interspersed in perfect layers. But it is also a good lunch spot where you can eat Sicilian pasta with fresh *sarde* (sardines) and wild fennel. There's also *timballo di anelletto* (pasta pudding) with tomato sauce and lots of cheese, Sicilian pizza *sfincione* and *caponata* – a sweet-and-sour vegetable mix with eggplant, celery and capers.

It's a good meeting place, especially on a rainy day. The tables are set right in the middle of the galleria Esedra. Perfect for an *aperitivo* and a bite. Reach the galleria from both Via Vittorio Emanuele Orlando or from Via Torino.

- **O** *Open every day 7am–11pm*
- **A** *Via Vittorio Emanuele Orlando 75; Center – near Roma Termini*
- **T** *+39 06 481 8660*
- **W** *www.pasticceriadagnino.com*

ENOTECA D'ORIO

A historic wine shop with a good selection. Later in the evening it becomes an authentic *aperitivo* bar with only Italian customers. Good wines on offer, around 6–7 euro for a glass. Canapés, small rice balls, salami and salted pizza-dough breadsticks are included in the price.

It's best on a summer evening with several tables outside. The easiest way to get here is via tram 3 or 19 from

Policlinico. Get off at stop Regina Margherita–Via Nomentana.

- **O** *Open every day 9am–11pm, except Sunday*
- **A** *Piazza Regina Margherita 9; Trieste*
- **T** *+39 06 442 50905*

CAVOUR 313

From October to November, this wine restaurant is one of my go-to places. It feels authentic, consistent and they have an enormous knowledge of wine. You can stop in and just have a quick glass at the bar or sit down and browse through the giant wine list that includes a thousand wines.

Hotel Mediterraneo
(p. 138)

For a long time they mostly served cold cuts and cheeses, the day's soup and lasagne. Today it's a complete restaurant: meatballs in white wine, grilled pork fillet with leek and chopped almonds and pistachios. The house *brasato* (beef roast) is a perfect choice with one of Piemonte's red wines like barolo or barbaresco. But here there is also fish, like *trota* (trout) baked in the oven with citrus fruits, to try with a wine like verdicchio from the Marche region.

- **O** *Open every day 12.30am–2.45pm, 6pm–11.30pm*
- **A** *Via Cavour 313; Monti*
- **T** *+39 06 678 5496*
- **W** *www.cavour313.it*

HOTEL FORUM

This hotel is nice in an old-fashioned way; the parquet floor really crackles. Take the elevator up to the fourth floor, where the restaurant is. One small staircase leads you up to the rooftop bar, one of the city's hidden gems, and the main reason to come here.

Paris gets the glory, but Rome's blue hour – when dusk falls – is unique and magical. Here you get a view over the Roman Forum and Capitoline Hill. The whole history of Rome spreads out before you while you enjoy a Campari, a Negroni, a glass of wine or the Italian upper-class sparkling franciacorta. The bar is relatively exclusive, which is reflected in the price list and the vintage Champagne. It's mostly just the hotel's international guests here. But you forget that immediately, because the Roman feeling is so strong. There aren't many tables, but I have never failed to get one. You can also book in reception or by

Angelo Di Blasio at Cavour 313

Valentina Cattani at Cavour 313

email. A must on a warm summer evening in the city.

O *Open every day 5.30pm–12am, rooftop*
   bar closed November–March and in
   bad weather
A *Via Tor de' Conti 25–30; Center –*
   adjacent to Via dei Fori Imperiali
T *+39 06 679 2446*
W *www.hotelforum.com*
E *info@hotelforum.com*

HOTEL MEDITERRANEO

One of Rome's primary and most beautiful examples of Art Deco architecture. For those interested in architecture, there is much to study here, like the white stairs of Carrara marble. The house with its ten floors is 164 feet (50 meters) high. The Bettoja family couldn't add more floors in the 1930s because if they had, the hotel would have been higher than St Peter's Basilica! Here you are at the highest point on the hill Esquiline.

The bar on the tenth floor, where it's never full, is magical at dusk in summer. The whole city along with St Peter's cupola stretches out in front of you. The place is neither trendy nor expensive; around 5 euro for a glass of the house wine with peanuts and chips is worth it for this view. And you won't be the slightest bit snobbily treated if you just come in for a glass. This is one of Rome's best bar addresses, known to very few. To eat on the terrace, which I have never done, will be considerably more expensive.

O *Open until 12am (bar)*
A *Via Cavour 15; Esquilinen*
T *+39 06 488 4051*
W *www.romehotelmediterraneo.it*

The view from Hotel Mediterraneo's rooftop terrace

HYBRIS

A hybrid art gallery and bar is the successful concept for this new place. Every other month there's new contemporary art with a small opening party. Otherwise, it's a bar with drinks, snacks and small plates. The space feels airy and spacious. There's an exciting murmur in the air, lots of Italians and a wide range of ages, from 30 to 60. There are charcuterie plates, lasagne, cannelloni, vegetarian couscous and beef tartare with teriyaki marinade and pink salt for those who are hungry. Sometimes they have jazz concerts; check the website. Hybris lies in the most authentic part of Trastevere near the Piazza in Piscinula.

O *Open every day 10am–2am*
A *Via della Lungaretta 164; Trastevere*
T *+39 06 943 76374*
W *www.hybrisartgallery.com*

∧ **Hybris – a bar in Trastevere**

IL GOCCETTO

One of the city's oldest wine bars, with personality and knowledgeable staff. The regulars, of which there are many and most are Italian, gather here in the evenings. Here there's no talk of *aperitivo*; you choose the wine you want by the glass and point at the snacks that lie on the counter: rolls of smoked salmon with creamy robiola cheese. I tried a version with sliced red peppers filled with tuna fillet. The snacks are small, but don't cost much either. There's also the salty pie *tiella* from Gaeta which normally is filled with octopus and tomatoes, but there's also a version with roasted escarole, capers and pine nuts. If there's a group of you, you can share the house large plate with bites of *antipasto del goccetto*.

The bar is for wine lovers. Few other wine bars have such an assortment of wines by the glass, a total of about

10 white wines and at least as many red, as well as Champagne. I drank an austere chablis and then returned to the Italian wines, like a verdicchio of Jesi from Marche. Good value and glasses are generously poured.

- **O** *Open Tuesday to Saturday 12pm–2.30pm, Monday to Saturday 6.30pm–12am*
- **A** *Via dei Banchi Vecchi 14; Center*
- **T** *+ 39 06 686 4268*
- **W** *www.ilgoccetto.com*

_____

IL VINAIETTO

A cute little wine bar with a whiff of the '60s about it. The place is easy to miss on the street behind the square Largo di Torre Argentina. It stands out however, with its low prices, around 4 euro for a glass of wine. It's good to bring along something to eat with your wine, so browse the quarter's food shops: pizza slices or bread and cold cuts. In this way it becomes a really inexpensive dinner, if you luck into a table! There are only four tables plus a few stools for seating.

In the evenings, most people hang around outside in the street with their wine. Marco and Giancarlo who run the place are real wine lovers. The second room doubles as a wine shop. It's totally ok to uncork one of the shop's red wines, which shows how much the owners value their guests. Here they don't add more than 5 euros for the bottle if you drink it on site. Good-value snacks like peanuts, chips or *taralli* (salted pretzels) are available.

- **O** *Open every day 10.30am–3pm, 6–11pm, except Sunday*
- **A** *Via del Monte della Farina 38; Center*
- **T** *+39 06 688 06989*

_____

NECCI DAL 1924

Pigneto is often described as the new Trastevere. It has become trendy, and everything that entails, with plenty of culinary daytrippers. Necci started as an ice-cream bar in the '20s. This is the neighborhood's meeting point, from early morning for breakfast and newspaper reading until far into the wee small hours. Here you can eat a light lunch, but it's primarily at 7-ish at night that the place rapidly fills up. That's when it's time for *aperitivo*. You can combine countless small dishes with a glass or a bottle of wine.

From the very first warm spring evening the large garden will fill up to the last table. There is a full dinner menu – not particularly varied, and it costs more than it merits. The easiest route here is tram 5 and 14 from Roma Termini to Piazzale Prenestino.

- **O** *Open every day 8am–1am*
- **A** *Via Fanfulla di Lodi 68; Pigneto*
- **T** *+39 06 976 01552*
- **W** *www.necci1924.com*

_____

692 SECRET GARDEN

Located at the city boundary where Porta Furba meets one of Rome's important aqueducts, "Felice" – often poetically mistranslated as "the happy water". Its name actually has to do with Felice Peretti either, who became Pope Sixtus V in the 1500s; which is to say, the aqueduct is new by Roman standards. The setting is unique, and in the evenings the old aqueduct is elegantly illuminated. The newly renovated restaurant section is worth trying, but this is a place for *aperitivo*, if you're looking for an authentic experience. It's open year-round, but this place is absolutely all about the warm summer evenings! Ten minutes' walk from the metro Porta Furba.

- **O** *Open for dinner from 7pm; aperitivo 6–9pm*
- **A** *Via Tuscolana 692; at the level of Pota Furba*
- **T** *+39 06 769 68667*

PASCUCCI

This place has been here for 80 years and is not the least bit dusty, but nor is it quite trendy. Pascucci shares a name with the owner family. The family lives by what they do, mindful of the fact that no other bar in Rome does anything quite similar. As early as the '50s they began making smoothies – fruit drinks that in Italian are called *frullati*. You choose what kind of fruit you want – strawberry, blueberry, banana, mango or papaya – which is mixed with ice and milk. Variations can be endless, with yoghurt added and the option to have whipped cream on top. It can be wise to opt for a proven combination like Amalfi: pear, apple, banana, lemon, milk and a splash of cherry juice. Incredibly nutritious and a bit strange compared to a typical milkshake. Ice-cream doesn't come across the threshold in this place.

This is not a bar where you sit down; rather, people slip hastily in and take their fresh fruit juice and then go on their way. Very popular, not least because a large glass with whipped fruit seldom costs more than around 4 euro.

- **O** *Open every day 6am–11pm, except Sunday*
- **A** *Via di Torre Argentina 20; Center*
- **W** *www.pascuccifrullati.it*

ROSATI

Two cafes, Canova and Rosati, have long existed in this large square with the city gates where Queen Kristina of Sweden first made her entry into the Eternal City in 1655. You must choose one, you cannot be a regular at both, according to Roman tradition. I have always gone to Rosati, mostly for a quick espresso at the counter in this beautiful 1920s cafe. Or grabbed a prosecco with a sandwich. It's more expensive to sit at the tables.

Earlier this was a traditional meeting place for young Romans, who parked their motorcycles next door and took a classic *aperitivo* consisting of a Campari and the house green olives. Now the square has become car-free and the tradition is gone. It's mostly international visitors here, but the location is distinctly Roman. In the

⌄ Rosati, historic cafe on Piazza del Popolo; an occasional red Ferrari manages to wind up here, even though the square is nearly car-free

Grilled salmon with a crust of finely chopped pistachios, served with black rice mixed with avocado at Molo 9/12 (p. 143)

Tasty shellfish pasta, *frutti di mare*

oval-shaped square a giant 3300-year-old obelisk – brought from Egypt by Pope Sixtus V in 1589 – meets Giuseppe Valadier's quirky 1800s-era architecture. As if this were not enough reason to stop here, there's also the church Santa Maria del Popolo with **Caravaggio's** (p. 170) famous paintings, a church that Dan Brown studied in minute detail for his famous novel *Angels and Demons*.

(O) *Open every day 7.30pm–12am*
(A) *Piazza del Popolo 4–5; Center*
(T) *+39 06 322 5859*
(W) *www.barrosati.com*

⌄ **Grilled tuna with crispy pork and garnished with black sesame seeds; a large portion for a starter at Molo 9/12 (p. 143)**

MOLO 9/12

Garbatella is an authentic neighborhood in Rome that tourists have not found their way to yet. It is a small area with charming multi-family apartment buildings; in short, a slightly more upscale version of the fascist-designed housing, often with large courtyards. This part of town was developed near the end of the 1920s, and it's teeming with exciting restaurants. Molo 9/12's owner, Emiliano Chierici, opened his restaurant here three years ago. He decided to call his place Molo 9/12 (*molo* means "pier") in order to emphasize that here you eat fish, not meat. The quality is high, while the prices are standard. We're not in the city center.

Grilled tuna with crispy pork on top and garnished with black sesame seeds is a delicious starter. The portion is so large that it could be a main dish. A paper cone of freshly deep-fried small squid is a more reasonably-sized starter and costs 8 euro. The house spaghetti with clams is a generous portion for 10 euro, as is *trofie* (macaroni) with grouper and grated lemon peel for 14 euro. Among the main dishes, we liked the beautiful presentation of a large piece of grilled salmon in a crust of finely chopped pistachio. The fish is served with black rice mixed with avocado. Simple and perfectly made. The wine list is sufficiently large, but contains only one pinot nero red. Garbatella is best reached with the metro B – the blue line – to Garbatella station. From here it's a 10-minute walk. Some of the streets in this neighborhood are small and winding. Make sure your cellphone battery is charged! An alternative that takes a little longer is bus 715 from Marcellus Theater adjacent to Piazza Venezia. The bus stops very close by. Disembark at the stop marked Rho.

- ⓞ *Open every day for lunch and dinner except Monday in winter; open every day for dinner only in summer*
- Ⓐ *Piazza Giovanni da Triora 9/12; Garbatella*
- Ⓣ *+ 39 33 480 58281*

SALOTTO 42

The model Malin Persson and her partner Damiano Mazzarella opened this trendy, cozy and cosmopolitan place in 2004. The place has managed to uphold a well-balanced mix of good music, the right people and a lighting system that dims with the evening light, as the volume goes up. When Malin and Damiano chose to move back to Skåne (in southern Sweden), many thought the place would change. It hasn't, most likely because they still own it.

Salotto has progressed, and a second location opened in 2016 in Copenhagen. Back at the original location, the day visitor

Swedish mammas with baby strollers have disappeared, as have the cinnamon buns. But the place is still tops, with perhaps Rome's best drinks. There's always something new to try: Raspberry Sage with vodka, lime, raspberry and sage; Cuban Manhattan made of rum flavored with figs, martini rosso and Angostura. Along with a drink, house snacks are included, either chips or peanuts. They also serve cold cuts and cheese, falafel and a croque monsicur. And what do you say to salted donuts with mortadella? In winter there's chocolate fondue that's eaten with fresh fruit and dry biscuits.

The best thing about the place is that it's never been too cool or snobby. As a rule there's no doorman, but it gets packed on Friday and Saturday nights. I have never encountered a similar bar whether in Rome, Stockholm or Milan. Outside the window is Emperor Hadrian's temple lit up in the car-free square. Salotto 42 is a must in Rome.

- ⓞ *Open every day 10am–2am*
- Ⓐ *Piazza di Pietra 42; Center*
- Ⓣ *+39 06 678 5804*
- Ⓦ *www.salotto42.it*

STRAVINSKIJ BAR

Hotel bars seldom make me happy. But Stravinskij isn't like the other places, nor is the hotel De Russie either, for that matter. Stravinskij has a special atmosphere that doesn't scream the word luxury; rather, the bar whispers of a subdued elegance and is a perfect meeting place for those who want to escape the crowd for an hour or two. Around 70 percent of the bar's guests come from abroad.

It is just as nice to sit indoors in the modern space where much of the decor is done in a warm gray color with exceptional golden detailing. In summer the large garden is an oasis where you can settle in with anything from an espresso to a drink. You can also try a smaller meal or one of the snacks normally provided: potato and root-vegetable chips, three kinds of large olives and a large glass full of vegetable sticks. The drinks list is 10 pages long with a special section for drinks made with vermouth and gin, as well as countless variations on the classic gin and tonic. We tried the house version of a Spritz: prosecco flavored with a secret concentration of red fruit, saffron, lemon and passionfruit – a light, fresh drink with a faint rose tint that, like nearly all the drinks, costs 22 euro. For those who are hungry there's a bar menu specially composed by the cook Fulvio Pierangelini.

O *Open every day 9am–1am*
A *Hotel De Russie, Via del Babuino 9; Center – adjacent to Piazza del Popolo*
T *+39 06 328 881*

―――――

THE FIDDLER'S ELBOW

This is Rome's first Irish pub. Properly smoky because it started as early as 1976, but today you can only smoke in the street. There are a lot of Irish pubs in the city, obviously many visitors want to take a break from all the wine bars. There's often good Italian beer, but proper dark Guinness you'd have to search for. In this bar where Irish memorabilia covers the walls your search can finally end.

The beer selection is extensive, from Guinness (stout) to Kilkenny (ale), Smithwicks (red ale) and Harp (lager). But also Becks, Carlsberg, Elephant (double malt) and Angelo (ale) – all on tap. The only Italian beer is Menabrea in a bottle and Peroni, which also makes a gluten-free beer. The shelves are lined with an assortment of whiskeys and Italian spirits. There might be a bottle of wine forgotten under the counter. The regulars are always friendly and many of them are Irish.

Go here for Saint Patrick's Day (March 17), and the place practically explodes in celebration and good spirits. The pub is just big enough so that it's fairly easy to get a table. On Wednesdays an Irish band plays live music in the room at the back.

O *Open every day 5pm–1am*
A *Via dell'Olmata 43; Esquiline – adjacent to Santa Maria Maggiore*
T *+39 06 487 2110*
W *www.thefiddlerselbow.com*

―――――

VESPER

One of the city's coziest new wine bars, this place fills up quickly. But the locals know to book a table at least a day before, as the place isn't huge. Here there are fun cocktails from a fantastic bartender and a good wine offering by both the glass and the bottle. There are more than just the usual snacks, including small plates like eggplant gratin, the day's lasagne, chicken, roast beef and medium salads. There are only a few tables outdoors. Vesper lies in an authentic and tourist-free neighborhood, 10 minutes' walk from the metro Bologna.

O *Open every day except Monday, 5pm–12.30am*
A *Piazza Massa Carrara 5; Nomentano*
T *+39 34 255 35344*
W *www.facebook.com/vesperroma*

―――――

CAFES

081 CAFÉ

From the outside this place looks like an ordinary, basic cafe with a few tables set out along a lively, well-trafficked street. But the espresso machine, the one that has an arm that the barista pulls down to brew the coffee, shows that here there is a true love of coffee.

That kind of machine requires a lot of manual attention and is therefore becoming increasingly rare. A shame, because the coffee it makes is superb. The place is Neapolitan through and through and uses only Kimbo coffee from Naples. The cafe's slogan is: "Accept no coffee from a stranger". The owner Gianluca Capuano radiates genuine southern Italian warmth, and by the blue-and-white decals along the walls you can see right away that his heart beats for his hometown football team, Napoli.

Beyond coffee, there are Neapolitan specialties like *sfogliatelle*, a sort of danish made of puff pastry and filled with fresh sweet ricotta cream, or the tart-pie *pastiera*. The name 081 refers to the area code for Naples.

O *Open every day 7.30am–6.30pm*
A *Via Merulana 83; Esquiline*

SANT'EUSTACHIO IL CAFFÈ

All the design here is original and untouched since the place opened in 1938. In the evenings it can get so full that it's hard to reach the counter. Romans mob the place because Sant'Eustachio is considered to have the city's best coffee. It serves around 4000 cups of coffee daily. The secrecy around it is great. Customers never see the coffee being made, and how the place's Gran Caffè Speciale gets so

XVII

ON ESPRESSO AND CAFE LATTE

First of all: forget about the cafe latte that you find in other countries. Latte exists in Italy, but I very rarely hear it ordered. It is almost a child's drink.

The other thing to remember is that there is not really an international cafe culture in Rome, where people sit and read newspapers and magazines for hours. The fine outdoor seating areas in piazzas are for drinking something other than coffee.

The velvety black espresso in Rome is, nine times out of ten, taken while standing at the bar, and it is just an espresso or, extremely rarely, a *doppio* (double). You can, of course, ask for something as complicated as having your espresso served *al vetro* (in a glass). You taste it better then, say the connoisseurs. But I don't believe that.

Drink many cappuccinos in the morning, but few Romans would order one after 11am. To sip one after lunch or dinner is blasphemy. A compromise, especially for those who are large cappuccino consumers and want happy stomachs, is to ask for a splash of foamed milk in the coffee. It's called a *macchiato*, which literally means "spotted". A *latte macchiato* is the direct opposite, a little black coffee in a large glass with warm foamed milk. Maybe it's this variation that definitively beat out cafe latte in Italy.

The options don't end there. A cappuccino can be *chiaro* (light) or *scuro* (dark), and if you want it without foam, *senza schiuma*. A straightforward cup of coffee is called a *caffè corretto* (coffee correct). You have to specify if you want something in it: grappa and brandy are the most common, but if you order *caffè mistral* you will automatically get anise liqueur in your coffee.

In summertime it's popular to have a *caffè freddo* (ice coffee). The coffee is pre-sweetened. In Rome it's extremely rare that you'd get your ordinary espresso with sugar, but in Naples it's normal. There the coffee is so strong that everyone has sugar in it, and if you don't want it sweetened you have to ask for a *caffè amaro*.

Traditions are strong. Starbucks has not yet dared to open and Nespresso hasn't gotten far, despite the fact that Italian resident George Clooney stars in its TV ads. Candy-sweet coffee has been slow to arrive, and it's popular to have a *crema* – sugar that's whipped with coffee into a thick cream – in a cup. But even hazelnut cream can be found, as well as chocolate. Variations with steamed milk and cocoa powder are known as *Marocchino* (Moroccan), and continue to be called that, especially in northern Italy.

To have a coffee in Italy is a rite of passage. Vendors exist in some office buildings, but they are used only in emergencies. Romans take a short break and go down to the bar.

The coffee is cheap. An espresso never costs more than 1 euro. Naturally a *macchiato* never costs more than an ordinary espresso, even though the milk prices in Italy are significantly higher than elsewhere.

creamy when it's served in a huge cup remains a mystery. The brewing machine that stands at the back against the counter even has a shield over the edge so that you can't see how the barista works. The coffee is creamy even without sugar and milk.

You can buy coffee beans to take home, and also fun little espresso brewers for two cups, coffee-flavored liqueur and candies like chocolate-covered coffee beans.

O *Open every day 8am–1am, Friday to Saturday until 1.30am*
A *Piazza di Sant'Eustachio 82; Center*
T *+39 06 688 02048*
W *www.santeustachioilcaffe.com*

CAFFÈ VERGNANO EATALY

Eataly is Rome's new food palace spread over three floors – nearly as large as an IKEA warehouse. Naturally coffee has an important place. Skip the coffee stand on the bottom floor and try instead the coffee market Vergnano on the second floor. This quality roastery comes from Piemonte, as does the whole slow food–movement that's behind Eataly.

There's a special coffee, Terre Alte, which is made from beans that grew on the high plateaus in Guatemala and Honduras. One of Rome's few coffee bars that still has the exclusive vertical Elektra Belle Epoque coffee machine in chrome, crowned with a large, glittering eagle.

A *Piazzale 12 ottobre 1492; Ostiense*
W *www.roma.eataly.it*

CANOVA TADOLINI

The sculptor Antonio Canova's studio from the early 1800s has been preserved and resurrected as a cafe. The studio was taken over by his apprentice Adamo Tadolini, whose family then worked in the studio for four generations, until 1967. Now you can knock back an espresso or eat lunch or dinner (relatively expensive) in this authentic artist's studio filled with hundreds of plaster casts of Canova's

❯ Sculptor Antonio Canova's studio today is the unique cafe Canova Tadolini, filled with several plaster casts of the artist's work

XVIII

THE COST OF SITTING DOWN

Waitstaff at coffee bars are always friendly. "Prego", they say, meaning please sit down. It's good to know that the prices are nearly always higher if you sit down. At the counter a regular coffee costs around 1 euro, even at slightly fancier places. But to sit down costs as a rule more than double, and significantly more at fancier places like along Via Veneto and Piazza Navona.

and the Tadolini family's models and sculptures. A unique place that Federico Fellini, who lived in the next block, especially loved.

- 🅞 *Open every day 8am–10.30pm*
- 🅐 *Via del Babuino 150; Tridente Center*
- 🅣 *+39 06 321 10702*
- 🅦 *www.canovatadolini.com*

GATSBY

An old clothing store has transformed into one of the city's hippest cafes. Much of the interior is intact from the '50s, the rest has been stylishly reconstructed by five coffee enthusiasts who opened the place in November 2016. Many of the shop's historic hats are still here, as is part of the sewing studio.

Here you can have your breakfast, sit and read the newspaper, and feed yourself on delicious sandwiches, or have a glass of wine in the evening. Lasagne is served, as

well as salad and fresh buffalo mozzarella. The perfect place for an *aperitivo* with snacks. Try the house variation on a Spritz, flavored with elderflower or rhubarb liqueur. Good value.

The square was once fairly rundown, but now the atmosphere is different. It's reputation has improved, not least thanks to the square's three permanent resident film directors, Paolo Sorrentino, Matteo Garrone and Abel Ferrara, who have become full-time Romans.

- 🅞 *Open every day 7.30am–12am, Saturday to Sunday until 2am*
- 🅐 *Piazza Vittorio Emanuele II 106; Esquiline*
- 🅣 *+39 06 693 39626*
- 🅦 *www.gatsby.cafe*

GRAN CAFFÈ LA CAFFETTIERA

An elegant cafe near the parliament buildings, where both politicians and business people knock back an espresso or take a seat at an outdoor table. The coffee is extra strong, like it usually is in the south, and a coffee bar with the same name also exists in central Naples. Here the machine is maintained and supervised carefully. The barista knows exactly how the coffee should be tamped down, also how tightly it should be packed. It's done totally manually before the brew arm is set on the machine. Sweet Neapolitan pastries like *sfogliatella*, *pasticciotto* and chocolate cake from Capri are perfect with an espresso.

- 🅞 *Open Monday to Friday 7.30am–9pm, Saturday 9am–9pm, Sunday 9am–10pm*
- 🅐 *Piazza di Pietra 65; Center*
- 🅦 *www.lacaffettieraroma.it*

PANELLA

Fresh danish pastries and croissants are served for breakfast at this bakery and cafe with a flurry of preserves, marmalades, spices, flour and quality pasta like Setaro. From 7pm *aperitivo* with a delicious buffet is available for around 20 euro.

- O *Open Monday to Saturday 8am–11pm, Sunday until 4pm*
- A *Via Merulana 54; Esquiline*
- W *www.panellaroma.com*

TAZZA D'ORO

Tazza D'Oro, the golden cup, is an historic coffee bar adjacent to the Pantheon. Since 1946 the Fiocchetto family has taught Romans what proper coffee is. Today it's the only place in Rome's center that still has permission to roast coffee beans on site. Here you'll find gourmet coffee Jamaica Blue Mountain, organic coffee from Java and coffee from Yemen called Queen of Sheba.

You can also buy whole beans or freshly ground coffee to take home. Beyond coffee, you can also try a semi-frozen dessert made of concentrated espresso and served with plenty of whipped cream – *granita al caffè*.

- O *Open Monday to Saturday 7am–8pm, Sunday 10.30am–7.30pm*
- A *Via degli Orfani 84; Center – near the Pantheon*
- W *www.tazzadorocoffeeshop.com*

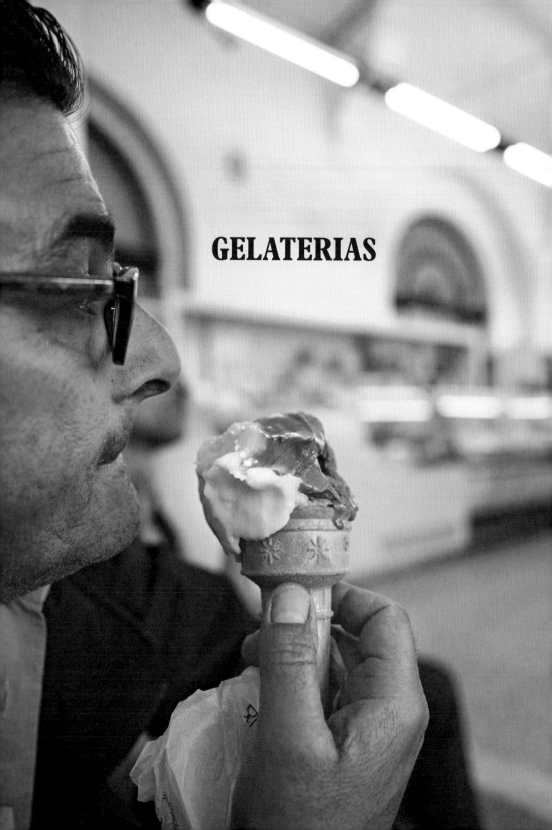

GELATERIAS

CAFFÈ DU PARC

Near the metro Piramide lies this little outdoor cafe, known for its concentrated and refreshing fruit-based ice-cream, *cremolati*. Today it is nearly alone in making this special dessert, where no other liquid is added. Strawberry, raspberry, *gelsi* (mullberry) and all imaginable citrus fruits are available. Tables are located ouside in the back; you can sit quietly here and relax.

(O) *Open every day during summer*
(A) *Viale della Piramide Cestia x Via Marmorata; Ostiense – near Porta San Paolo*

FASSI – PALAZZO DEL FREDDO

Enjoy a cone or ice-cream pastry in a unique location. Fassi's ice palace is a piece of cultural history that started as early as 1928. The giant eatery was previously a depot for horse-drawn carriages. The space is like a giant ballroom, where people settle themselves down during the early afternoon to eat ice-cream at the stylish marble tables with black-and-white mottling – a pattern that resembles a perfect *stracciatella*. Here there weren't just 36 flavors, but also several ice-cream pastries. The founder, Giovanni Fassi, was originally a baker and his great-great-granddaughter Andrea guards family recipes, including chocolate-covered *sanpietrini*, which look like miniature versions of Rome's paving stones. Grandmother Giuseppina's cassata are specially balanced with hazelnut, pistachio and candied fruit. At the counter are also perfect *tramezzini*, grilled three-corner sandwiches that exist in all of Rome's bars, but here the sandwich bread has been replaced by frozen sugar cookies filled with forest-berry ice-cream.

Fassi – Palazzo del Freddo

On the walls hang posters from the '30s – ads for Fassi's patented, and at the time revolutionary, new *telegelato*. Yep, Fassi was the first person to send ice-cream around the world in special packaging with dry ice.

(O) *Open every day except Monday*
(A) *Via Principe Eugenio 65–67; Esquiline*
(W) *www.palazzodelfreddo.it*

CAFFÈ DI NOTO

A little ice-cream bar with genuine flavors from Sicily. Pistachio, almond, *zuppa Inglese* flavored with rum and Palermo's chocolate cake *sette veli* (seven layers) but as an ice-cream version. The smallest serve

an aftertaste of dried raisin and mild cinnamon. It's an ice-cream to eat every day, if you can!

Ⓐ *Via dei Gracchi 272; Prati*
Ⓦ *www.gelateriadeigracchi.it*

GELATERIA SANTA MARIA MAGGIORE
This newcomer has a large selection that has already won several prizes. Try the *apfelstrudel* – creamy vanilla meets apple, cinnamon and crumble topping. Also a perfect *nocciola* – hazelnut and pistachio. The Mojito ice is also worth sampling.

Ⓐ *Via Cavour 93–95; Esquiline*

⌄ **If you don't want to have a cone, you can at many places have ice-cream in a *brioscina* (sliced sweet bun), as is a tradition in Sicily**

costs 2.50 euro and it is large. If you want whipped cream on top it costs extra.

Ⓐ *Piazza Colonna 356; Center – along Via del Corso*

GELATERIA DEI GRACCHI
The flavors here vary depending on the time of year and which fresh ingredients are available. All are good, and many are utterly sublime. A good trick for choosing the best flavour is to look inside the counter and check which flavors are nearly gone. I hesitated forever before I finally chose meringue with pistachio. Yummy. The apple ice-cream is a little slice of heaven; both sweet and fruity fresh with

GIOLITTI

A must! Here there's still an elegant salon with table service by livery-clad waitstaff. New additions among the flavors include *Vacanze Romane*, named after the film with Audrey Hepburn and made with pear, walnut, figs and caramel.

Ⓐ *Via degli Uffici del Vicario 40; Center*
Ⓦ *www.giolitti.it*

SAN CRISPINO

Nanni Moretti's favorite; the Italian director has put this ice-cream maker in several of his films and the ice-cream is in a class by itself.

A few years ago, a Berlin Wall fell here in Rome's ice-cream world – San Crispino brought in *coni* (cones). If you asked earlier if you could have ice-cream in a cone instead of a *coppa* (cup), you would get the snobby answer: "We put our entire soul into the quality with the very best ingredients. So we can't serve our ice-cream in a cone that's laced with preservatives". Today a sign at the counter informs you that these are organic cones. Feel free to enjoy their mild vanilla ice-cream spiked with honey from Sardinia, or a perfect mix of walnut, fig and dates. Many locations in the city.

Ⓐ *Piazza della Maddalena 3; Center – near the Pantheon*
Ⓦ *www.ilgelatodisancrispino.com*

SORA MARIA

Sora Maria is a *grattachecca*, the simplest form of ice-cream shop that exists in Italy. On the beach you used to see a man pulling a wagon who shaves an ice block and fills a mug. Then he pours concentrated juice over the shaved ice. Maria Facchini renewed this tradition when she opened her kiosk here in 1933. Today it's run by her daughter Gabriella.

This is refreshing shaved-ice, in a mug, that's blended with fruit – perfect for a hot summer day. I tried a *dissetante*; it was thirst-quenching with orange juice, lemon and coconut, blended with fruit chunks. "Epicurean's favorite" consists of cherry, tamarind and orange garnished with cherry, lemon and forest berries. In total this little kiosk has over 50 different kinds of juice to choose from. Sora Maria is one of the last kiosks to keep this typical Roman tradition going, and the line on a warm summer night can be very long.

Ⓞ *Open every day April to October 3.30–8.30pm, 9pm–12am, Sunday from 7pm*
Ⓐ *Via Trionfale x Via Bernardino Telesio; Trionfale – near the Vatican*

Ⓘ

XIX ITALIAN GELATO – THE WORLD'S BEST ICE-CREAM

No pretext is more common for a date in Rome than the obvious question: "Shall we go out and have an ice-cream together?" Ice-cream is popular to the extent that it often dominates the nightlife in Rome. The city's large ice-cream circuit goes from the Trevi Fountain over to the Pantheon and down to Piazza Navona. After a flaming-hot summer day comes the first evening breeze. That's when the narrow alleys in the city center fill up with ice-cream-loving tourists and Romans alike. Forget the wine bars, clubs and discos. The biggest fun in Rome is to walk around licking a cone of ice-cream under a black-velvet sky.

SORA MIRELLA

The city's oldest ice-cream stand sits alongside the bridge Ponte Cestio, which links Trastevere. to Tiber Island. Originally opened in 1915, before its jubilee in 2000 the community gave the owners permission to make this kiosk a little larger.

Here it's all about finely ground, refreshing shaved-ice, *grattachecca*, flavored with juice and fresh fruit. There's a large selection, and masses of people on a warm summer evening. It's a kiosk that has even been visited by Michelle Obama.

Ⓞ *Open every day in summer 7am–2am, in winter 7am–7pm; closed January to February*
Ⓐ *Lungotevere degli Anguillara; along the Tiber near Tiber island*

VENCHI

When the historic chocolate business Venchi ventured into the ice-cream world 100 years ago, the world's most delicious hybrid was born. Along the huge wall behind the ice-cream counter flows a chocolate waterfall – 770 pounds (350 kilograms) of liquid chocolate blended with olive oil. A delicious, fragrant presentation!

There are many ice-cream flavors here, from *Azteko* made only of water and 82-percent pure chocolate, to creamy *Cuor di Cacao* which includes milk and cream. In *Giandiutto* chocolate is interspersed with hazelnuts from the business's home region of Piemonte. Venchi's famous *Nougatine* – pralines with cocoa, almonds and caramel – also exist in ice-cream form. Sinfully good and seriously addictive.

Fruit-based ice-creams here are few. But the mango ice-cream is the perfect flavor complement to chocolate, at least in my cone.

There are also crepes that you can get with liquid chocolate and your choice of ice-cream inside. This is the city's largest Venchi shop and many people also buy a good assortment of the chocolate-maker's pralines to take home. Smaller shops are on Via della Croce 25 and Via degli Orfani 87 near the Pantheon and at Roma Termini.

Ⓞ *Open every day 10am–12.30am*
Ⓐ *Via del Corso 335; Center*
Ⓣ *+39 06 678 4698*
Ⓦ *www.venchi.com*

FOOD SHOPS

Midday siesta-closing is unusual in Rome these days. But some of the older stores keep the tradition and are closed from 1 or 2pm until 4 or 5pm. They are generally also closed on Sundays.

ANTICA CACIARA

This is a historic cheese shop that opened in the year 1900. As early as 6am in the morning the owner Roberto Polica is on the go; that's when the ultra fresh ricotta cheese made of sheep's milk, which was curdled that same morning, is delivered. Polica is 68 years old but he fortunately has no plans to step back. His son has already said no to taking over his father's 14-hour-long work days. Polica works hard, making panini with different toppings when a whole group of tourists come into the shop – something that a lot of shops today will flatly refuse to do. There's a black-waxed Roman pecorino to grate over spaghetti *all'amatriciana*. There are also meat dishes to go with the pasta, like *pancetta* and *guanciale* from Umbria.

O *Open every day 7am–9pm*
A *Via San Francesco a Ripa 140; Trastevere*
W *www.anticacaciara.it*

ANTONIO MICOCCI

There's only cheese in this family-run shop but it has the most variety, from northern Italian gorgonzola to peppery saffron cheese from Sicily.

O *Open every day 8.30am–7.30pm*
A *Via Collina 16; Pinciano*

BISCOTTIFICIO INNOCENTI

A bakery that primarily makes dry biscuits with craftsman's skill in a nine-meter-long oven. Biscotti to go with red wine and cookies made of cornflakes and chocolate remain its specialties. The bakery has a special unaffected atmosphere and, naturally, is family-run. Stefania Innocenti is the third generation of her family to run the business.

O *Open Monday to Saturday 8am–8pm, Sunday 9.30am–2pm*
A *Via della Luce 21; Trastevere*

COGLIONI di MULO
€ 22,00
AL KG

PALLE del NONNO
€ 22,00
AL KG

The *coglioni di mulo* (mule's balls) have a smooth surface, while the *palle di nonno* (granddad's balls) look more rough. Both are made of the finest parts of the pig and have a little white strip of fat inside

FINOCCHIONA TOSCANA   BRESAOLA   LONZA   COPP NO

BOCCIONE

A historic bakery in the city's old Jewish quarter that maintains tradition. Jewish pizza is a very sweet, oven-baked cake with candied citrus and raisin. The only thing it has in common with Italian pizza is that it's cut into slices. There are also cookies here; the best are *visciole*, pies with ricotta and amarelle. Why the aunties who work here have such a hard time cracking a smile, I don't know. Ignore the attitude and enjoy the cakes.

- Ⓞ *Open Monday to Thursday 8am–7pm, Friday until 1pm*
- Ⓐ *Via del Portico d'Ottavia 1; Il Ghetto*

CASTRONI

The city's largest grocery store where risotto rice, pistachios, almonds from Bronte in Sicily and pickled sardines are a good buy. They have nearly everything, except for fresh produce. There's another shop at Via Nazionale 71.

- Ⓞ *Open Monday to Saturday 8.30am–8pm, Sunday 9.30am–8pm*
- Ⓐ *Via del Portico d'Ottavia 1; Il Ghetto*

DELIZIE DI CALABRIA

Tonino Ciardullo is a brilliant ambassador for his southern Italian home region of Calabria. This store is small but has an enormous amount to offer and a unique selection: dried and fresh bolete mushrooms from the forests around Serra San Bruno and the high-elevation area Sila; also, dried and finely ground red *peperoncino*, and even some spiced tomato sauce that you put directly on bruschetta. *'Nduja* from Spilinga is a fresh and spreadable strong salami to eat with bread,

but it can also be used in pasta sauce. Try the tiny fish *neonata* (whitebait), marinated with chilis; this specialty has many other names like *rosamarina* or *sardella*. The salami *soppressata*, strongly or lightly spiced, is another good product to buy and take home.

The region is also known for unusual liqueurs made of *cedro* (thick-sliced citrus fruit) or licorice, and produced in Rossano. I often buy smoked aged ricotta cheese from the Sila mountains, made of sheep's milk. Perfect to sprinkle over a pasta with lamb ragu.

P.S. Above the store hangs a plaque in memory of the film director Mario Monicelli (1915–2010) who lived in this building.

O *Open every day 9am–9pm*
A *Via dei Serpenti 30, Monti*
T *+39 33 847 23822*

DROGHERIA INNOCENZI

There are no drugs sold here, but there's an exciting range of both Italian and international groceries. A unique shop.

O *Open every day, closed for siesta 1.30–5pm, Saturday open mornings only*
A *Via Natale del Grande 31; Trastevere*

EATALY

These days it exists even in Stockholm, but in Rome, Eataly is a giant food warehouse spread over four floors with gourmet restaurants and smaller eateries with different specialties. There's chocolate from **Venchi** (p. 161)and delicious pistachio cream to buy and take home. Try *piadina* (salted crepes) from Emilia with prosciutto and *squacquerone* (fresh creamy soft cheese). There's also a good fresh-food counter with fish, meat, fresh pasta, fruit and vegetables. And a large wine

selection where Piemonte dominates, but also many good rosé wines from Apulia.

- Ⓞ *Open every day 10am–12am*
- Ⓐ *Piazzale XII Ottobre 1492; Ostiense – in the connection to metro Piramide*
- Ⓦ *www.roma.eataly.it*

ELITE
A good, quality-conscious shop with a large charcuterie and cheese counter, and an enormous range. You can get anything you buy vacuum-packed free of charge, ready for the trip home. There's a large selection of pasta from small local producers with solid traditions. Also fun groceries, marmalades and delicious truffle products from Piedmont.

- Ⓞ *Open every day except Sunday*
- Ⓐ *Via Cavour 232; Esquiline*

IL MERCATO CENTRALE
Many of Rome's food markets have languished. The cheaper supermarkets have also disappeared from the capital. And certain markets have adapted to tourists, which means that fresh produce has given way to colorful pasta, preserves and marmalades. That makes it all the more fun that a large part of Rome's train station was transformed a couple of years ago into a market hall. It functions both as both a supermarket and as an eatery. Although here we're justified in talking about the eatery in the plural.

Mercato Centrale consists of around 20 food stations, from ham and sausages to cheese, wine, coffee and chocolate. There's bread and pizza by the slice by the guru **Gabriele Bonci** (p. 109) whose operation is constantly expanding. The Galluzzi family who runs the fish shop on the Esquiline has a counter with fresh bright-red shrimp and all possible types of fish. Most of it is grilled instead of being deep-fried. Choose your own meat for the barbecue: chianina beef from Tuscany, pork, chicken or salsiccia. The meat is express-grilled and served with oven-baked potatoes and salad. Even vegetarians and vegans have their options, with good alternative burgers.

There are also pastries and ice-cream here. And of course Stefano Calligari has a counter. He is famous in Rome's pizza world with places like **Sforno** and **Tonda** (p. 111 for both), and has developed the hybrid *trapizzini*. The name is a mix of Rome's three-cornered sandwiches, *tramezzini*, and pizza. *Trapizzini* is baked pizza dough that is opened and stuffed with filling. It's good with tongue in green sauce or with *baccalà* and red pepper.

In the vegetable stand, rinsing artichokes at high speed, I met Alessandro Conti. He is a fourth-generation owner of a market stand at the central Campo dei Fiori. These days he thinks that working with vegetables has become more prestigious, now that he's moved into the market hall.

The nicest thing about Mercato Centrale is that you can settle down exactly where you like and there are common drink stations with a large range of beer, wine and mineral water. The brains behind the project is Umberto Montano, and for many years he's had a well-known restaurant in Florence. In 2015 he transformed Florence's historic market San Lorenzo into a market hall with places to eat. A year later he repeated the concept at Roma Termini. Thanks to him, some new culinary energy has come in to Roma Termini and given both Romans and travelers an alternative to all the sad standard sandwiches.

- Open every day 7am–12am
- Via Giolitti 36; Roma Termini station
- www.mercatocentrale.it/roma

LE LEVAIN
In the middle of Trastevere, Italian Giuseppe Solfrizzi has opened a French boulangerie. Beyond bread, quiche and croissants with Italian prosciutto there are also delicious pastries. I tried a *tartellette* with passionfruit and a cheesecake with raspberries. The place quickly becomes addictive and it's worth sampling the whole range of treats. The fact that this baker practiced in Paris for a long time shows in the flavors.

There are a few chairs for enjoying your treats here. Coffee is served, but only in paper cups. This place is a must, primarily if you think Italian pastries tend to be too sweet. There's even a really good sandwich here, on house-baked bread of course.

- Open Monday to Saturday 8am–8.30pm, Sunday 9am–6.30pm
- Via Luigi Santini 22–23; Trastevere
- www.lelevainroma.it

NORCINERIA IACOZZILLI
A historic grocery with hands-on service. Buy your *pecorino Romano* from the historic brand Brunelli, which sets its cheese not in brine, but rather manually salts it, which gives it the perfect flavor for Roman pasta dishes.

- Open Monday to Saturday 9am–1pm, 4.30–8.30pm
- Via Natale del Grande 15; Trastevere

SELLI INTERNATIONAL FOOD STORE
From outside this place looks like a Chinese boutique. But it's been Italian-owned since the start, with unique specialties: basmati rice and countless Italian beans and legumes. Everything's in bulk. There are giant dates from Israel, but also unusual Italian specialties like black lentils and black rice. The best buy is pine nuts that smell like resin. They're good to eat as is, but are even tastier when roasted and mixed in a salad or in a pasta dish with vegetables. Here you can be sure that they come from the large pine forest in San Rossore outside of Pisa.

The store also has spices, unusual teas and special ingredients for making Thai, Indian or Japanese food. A little shop that is a delight to browse in.

- Open Monday to Saturday 9.30am–1.30pm, 4–8pm
- Via dello Statuto 28–30; Esquiline

VOLPETTI
This little family shop is the city's number one food temple, with a quality range, often from small producers. Wild boar salami, unique cheeses and good wines. Also ready-made small meals and pies.

- Open Monday to Wednesday 8.30am–2pm, 4.30–8.15pm; Thursday to Saturday 8.30am–8.15pm
- Via Marmorata 47; Testaccio
- www.volpetti.com

XX CARAVAGGIO'S DARKNESS AND LIGHT

A lifetime is not enough, either to see or feel Rome in full. If there's any place where you can get sick of art, monuments, fountains, cloisters, catacombs, ancient ruins, museums, parks, aqueducts, bridges, temples and not least churches, it's Rome. This book deals with food. So why write about Caravaggio? Well, because I love Caravaggio! And because you might need a little break from all the food.

He was born in 1571 as Michelangelo Merisi but was soon renamed Caravaggio, which was the name of his parents' home county south of the city of Bergamo in Lombardy. New findings show that he was very likely born in Milan, where he was baptized.

Caravaggio was a painter of light and darkness like no other, and of course formed his own art movement. He was a great colorist, blending his own colors. When someone recently wanted to reproduce a digital copy of *The Birth of Jesus* that Caravaggio had painted (the painting was stolen from Palermo in 1969 and has never been recovered) people analyzed the colors in other contemporary work. Caravaggio's deep blacks, which make the other colors in the painting explode, are an exactly balanced blend of green, blue and brown.

Caravaggio often painted himself into his artwork, for example as the Philistine warrior Goliath's severed head which King David holds up triumphantly. But often he's a witness, welcoming us into the scene, like when he painted *The Betrayal of Christ*, when Judas betrayed Jesus with a kiss – there stands Caravaggio, in the background, to the far right of the painting, holding up a lantern so we can see the scene.

In Rome, where he lived a long time, Caravaggio left many of his works. In the Galleria Borghese, aside from the previously mentioned *David with the Head of Goliath* there's a dramatic Madonna with baby Jesus and a snake on the floor. Also there is his painting of a young Bacchus who had probably drunk too much and the painting *Boy with a Basket of Fruit* – two homoerotic motifs that Caravaggio returned to many times.

In Palazzo Barberini there are two very famous paintings: the beautiful young Narcissus who saw himself reflected in a spring and fell in love with his own face; and the painting where Judith decapitates Holofernes – a story that was reproduced in Judith's book, a supplement to the Old Testament, but that never actually took place. The Vatican museum's painting gallery has only one Caravaggio, but it's one of the more magnificent paintings that shows the burial of Christ.

Most of Caravaggio's work is still in the city's big churches. In Santa Maria del Popolo he rendered two moments from the lives of the apostles Peter and Paul who both died in Rome. One painting shows how Paul, who at first persecuted the Christians, repented on the road to Damascus. The other shows Peter's martyrdom, when he was crucified upside down.

Caravaggio's most important complete work is in the French church San Luigi dei Francesi between the Pantheon and Piazza Navona. Here Caravaggio has painted a whole chapel in honor of Cardinal Matteo Contarelli's memory because he was a major patron of Caravaggio's. Therefore the paintings deal with the Apostle Matthew, the disciple who collected taxes. In three paintings Matthew's life is depicted: his calling, his meeting with the angel and his martyrdom.

It is *The Calling of St Matthew* on the far left wall that fascinates me the most. In the painting we are in a room with people around a large table. In my memory I thought for a long time that it was a wine cellar, that a glass stood on the table and that they were playing cards. Totally wrong! Jesus who has a barely visible halo comes into the room and points at Matthew, who is painted as two people: a very young boy and an old man with a full beard.

This painting holds a lot of meaning for Pope Francis too. During the 2013 conclave (the pope's selection in the Sistine Chapel), the then Argentine cardinal Jorge Mario Bergoglio (now Pope Francis) thought about Matthew, who in Caravaggio's painting sits far away, near a table full of money. He looks down at the table to avoid Jesus' gaze.

"It is Matthew's gesture that affects me, he holds tightly to the money as if he wants to say: No, not me! No, the money is mine! And here I [Pope Francis] stand, a sinner on whom the Lord has let his eyes fall. That was also what I answered when they asked if I accepted having been chosen as Pope", said Pope Francis in an interview with the Jesuit newspaper *La Civiltà Cattolica*.

Caravaggio did not exactly live by the Church's rules. On the contrary, he was in many fights and brawls; he was arrested and locked up several times; and he lived a sexually adventurous life and possibly consorted with both men and women, many of whom were prostitutes.

In 1606 Caravaggio killed Ranuccio Tomassoni in a dispute over the female prostitute Tillide Melandroni, who both Caravaggio and Ranuccio had their eye on. The Church forgave and accepted Caravaggio's life in the end, no doubt because of his divine painting, but after the murder he had to leave Rome.

The Church however did not accept all of his paintings. In 1605–06 he painted the death of the Virgin Mary. Caravaggio chose to drape Mary in a purple mantle – and thereby deliberately broke with the traditional chaste blue color. Mary's feet and legs are bare and the dress reveals a round stomach. The model was a prostitute who drowned herself in the Tiber in Rome. She may have been pregnant. The painting cannot be seen in Rome, though, because it was rejected by the Church, so Napoleon snapped it up in the 1800s and it was forever lost to Italy. It now hangs in the Louvre.

ⓘ

RESTAURANT PHRASEBOOK

Vorrei prenotare un tavolo per due per le ore venti di stasera. Ci sono ancora posti fuori?
I would like to reserve a table for two at 8pm this evening. Is there a place outdoors?

Avete un menu? Posso vederlo?
Do you have a menu? Could I have a look at it?

Scusi possiamo ordinare?
Excuse me, may we order?

Quali sono le vostre specialità? Cosa consiglia?
What are your specialties? What do you recommend?

E possibile avere una mezza porzione?
Is it possible to have a half-portion?

Io sono vegetariano, quali piatti avete?
I'm a vegetarian, which dishes can I choose from?

Possiamo provare il vino della casa? Un quartino per cominciare grazie.
Can we try the house wine? A quarter-liter to start with, please.

Posso avere un calice di vino?
May I have a glass of wine?

Vorrei acqua minerale gassata/liscia.
I would like mineral water with/without bubbles.

Che birra avete alla spina?
What beers do you have on tap?

**Niente antipasti grazie.
Prendiamo direttamente
un secondo.**
No starters, please. We'll go
straight to the main dishes.

**Vorrei la mia carne al
sangue/cottura media/
ben cotta.**
I would like the meat cooked
rare/medium/well-done.

**Possiamo avere sale e pepe
e olio e aceto per favore.**
Could we have salt and
pepper and oil-and-
vinegar, please?

**Il pesce è fresco o è
surgelato?**
Is the fish fresh or frozen?

**La pizza viene cotta nel
forno a legna?**
Do you make the pizza in a
wood-fired oven?

**La pizza è bruciata, potete
gentilmente rifarla?**
The pizza is burnt, can you
do anything about it for me?

**Due carciofi alla Romana
per favore!**
Two artichokes the Roman
way, please!

**Come contorno vorrei delle
patate al forno/spinaci/
puntarelle.**
I would like oven-baked
potatotes/spinach/salad
sprouts as a side.

**Il piatto era squisito, lo dica
al cuoco mi raccomando.**
This dish is exquisite, please
give our compliments to
the chef.

I dolci sono fatti in casa?
Are the desserts homemade?

**Un cono medio con
cioccolato e fragola con
panna grazie.**
I would like a medium
cone with chocolate and
strawberry plus whipped
cream, please.

INDEX

Published in 2019 by Hardie Grant Travel, a division of
Hardie Grant Publishing
First published in 2018 by Natur & Kultur, Sweden
Original title: Rom för Foodisar

Hardie Grant Travel (Melbourne)
Building 1, 658 Church Street
Richmond, Victoria 3121

Hardie Grant Travel (Sydney)
Level 7, 45 Jones Street
Ultimo, NSW 2007

www.hardiegrant.com/au/travel

A catalogue record for this
book is available from the
National Library of Australia

Rome for Food Lovers
ISBN 9781741176612

10 9 8 7 6 5 4 3 2 1

Publisher
Melissa Kayser
Project editor
Megan Cuthbert
Translator
Becky Ohlsen
Editor
Alison Proietto
Editorial assistance
Aimee Barrett and Rosanna Dutson
Typesetting
Megan Ellis
Prepress
Megan Ellis and Splitting Image Colour Studio

Printed in China by 1010 Printing International Limited

The images on pages 53, 96 and 144 are copyright Alamy Stock Photo.